I0459405

TELL THEM

Anyway

---

*The Message That
Changed Everything*

SHERRY DEPERNO

Copyright © 2025 by Sherry DePerno

All rights reserved. No part of this book may be used or reproduced by any means, graphic, electronic or mechanical, including photocopying, recording, taping or by any information storage retrieval system, without the written permission of the author, except in the case of brief quotations embodied in reviews. Deliberate use of this work for AI training is prohibited.

The author's health journey as shared in this book is her personal experience and is not meant to be taken as medical advice. Your decisions regarding medical care are your own.

Paperback ISBN 978-1-960007-84-1

Published by
Orison Publishers, Inc.
PO Box 188
Grantham, PA 17027
www.OrisonPublishers.com

Unless otherwise indicated, all Scripture quotations are taken from The Holy Bible, New International Version® NIV® Copyright © 1973, 1978, 1984, 2011 by Biblica, Inc. Used by permission. All rights reserved worldwide.

Scripture quotations marked ESV are taken from the ESV® Bible (The Holy Bible, English Standard Version®), copyright © 2001 by Crossway, a publishing ministry of Good News Publishers. ESV Text Edition: 2025. The ESV text may not be quoted in any publication made available to the public by a Creative Commons license. The ESV may not be translated in whole or in part into any other language. Used by permission. All rights reserved.

To contact the author, write:
Sherry DePerno
9169 River Road, Suite 3
Marcy, NY 13403
TellThemAnyway.com

I dedicate this book to:

My husband, Rob, who has loved me since we were 15 years old. You have stood by me through every wild idea and loved me at my best—and my worst.

My son Michael, who opened my eyes to a deeper view of God, helping me see beyond what I had known.

My son Matthew, who taught me courage—to be unafraid and true to myself.

My mom, Denise, an inspiring example of unwavering faith. You were the first to show me how to pray and trust in God, and I am who I am because of your love and guidance.

My dad, Harold ("Butch"), who showed me bravery and the strength to speak my mind. You made me feel deeply loved, and I always knew you were proud of me.

My friend and Bible-study leader Robin, whose wisdom, encouragement, and unwavering support played a pivotal role in my spiritual journey. Thank you for walking beside me.

The other members of my Bible study: Adrienne, our leader, along with Jenn, Tina, Patty, Krystal, Mary, Karylanne, and Roxanne, who listened, encouraged, and nurtured my growth as a Christian and as a person. I am deeply grateful. I love you all.

And my friend Dave, who encouraged me to stay connected with Redeemer Church and supported me as I sought a deeper relationship with God.

Contents

Chapter One – Never Satisfied 1

Chapter Two – The Bible's Power 11

Chapter Three – Going Deeper 23

Chapter Four – Looking Good... 29

Chapter Five – My Encounter 35

Chapter Six – Proof 41

Chapter Seven – More Blessings.. 51

Chapter Eight – The Enemy.. 61

Chapter Nine – COVID-19..77

Chapter Ten – Next Steps 83

Chapter Eleven – Not Quite the End..................................... 87

Chapter One
Never Satisfied

I spent my life chasing success, and by most standards, I caught it. I built multiple businesses, had money in the bank, traveled, won local and national awards, and earned the respect of my community. I married my high school sweetheart, and after 30 years of marriage, we are still in love and would do anything for each other. We raised two incredible sons, Michael and Matthew, who continue to make us proud. I also share an unbreakable bond with my parents and extended family.

On the outside, I had it all: a beautiful home, cars, toys, and everything extra. My ultimate goal was to own a beach house by the ocean, and my husband, Rob, and I were already browsing properties. So, this was it, right? I had reached the finish line of success.

Then why was there this nagging feeling that even if I got that beach house, it wouldn't be enough?

What I didn't understand then was that success and wholeness are not the same. I thought reaching my goals would make me feel complete. It didn't.

But an encounter with God did. That changed everything. I've heard people say that God often chooses the most unlikely individuals to act through so that His presence is unmistakable.

If you knew me, you'd know that talking about God was the last thing I'd ever do. As a business owner, I followed a strict rule: no talk of politics or religion.

Sure, I believed in God, but that part of my life was private, something I only shared with my family and closest friends.

Then God flipped my world upside down. He made Himself so undeniable in my life that I couldn't stay silent anymore. Over the course of a week in May 2024, He showed up in ways that left no room for doubt. He visited me. He healed me. And He completely transformed me.

***

Rob and I built Advanced Tool Inc., a global manufacturing business we purchased from my parents, who lived a true rags-to-riches story. When I was a baby, we were dirt poor. My mom would dig through couch cushions for spare change to buy powdered milk for my sister and me. Dad, a tool and cutter grinder, was constantly being laid off, so he started a resharpening business in our garage in Sauquoit, New York. Together, he and Mom grew that garage business into a million-dollar company.

At 16, I got my first taste of the family business—and it didn't go well. My parents fired me because I was a terrible employee with a bad attitude. I wanted to work only when I felt like it and do only what I wanted to do. Getting fired was the best thing they did for me. They told me I needed to grow up and find a real job.

So that's what I did. I learned quickly that the real world had its own set of rules. After a few years and some college experience, I returned to the family business, more mature and ready to contribute.

That's when I realized just how tough running a small business can be—especially a family business. I watched my parents go without paychecks when times were tough, and Dad always struggled to find skilled workers.

Around that time, I was dating Rob, and my dad needed help putting a roof on the building. Rob volunteered, and Dad, impressed by his work ethic, asked me how I'd feel about hiring him. We had a family meeting to discuss the risks if Rob and I broke up, but ultimately, Dad decided to hire him.

A few years later, I married him. So now I was working alongside my parents and my high school sweetheart-turned-husband. Rob, however, had the toughest spot. He was determined to prove to everyone in the company that he wasn't getting any special treatment from my dad. He earned his way to the top and eventually became Dad's right-hand man.

Years into the business, I saw a storm brewing. My dad was the primary salesperson, constantly bringing in work. Still, the jobs were becoming more complex, requiring highly skilled toolmakers—who were becoming harder and harder to find. We tried to hire and train from within, but nothing stuck. Rob, who had been managing the shop floor, would tell me how he and just one other guy were doing most of the work. I could see it: this wasn't sustainable. Something had to give.

Two books changed the direction of our business: *The E-Myth* by Michael E. Gerber and *Good to Great* by Jim Collins. Collins challenged me to build a company that excelled at something so specific and so great that we could be the best in the world. I was up for the challenge.

I got serious about the numbers. I analyzed every cutting tool we made, every service we offered, and I dug into the data to see which products were most profitable and most valuable to our customers. Carbide end mills stood out. For those unfamiliar with it, an end mill is an industrial cutting tool used across industries like aerospace, automotive, medical, and defense.

I realized that if we focused on mastering this one product—rather than trying to be everything to everyone—we could simplify training, sharpen our expertise, and grow the business.

And we did it. Today, no one can custom manufacture an end mill for a specific industrial application and deliver the performance and cost savings that we do. We've outperformed—and taken business from—some of the biggest names in our industry, which are billion-dollar global giants. We're David up against Goliath, and there's no better feeling than winning against them.

I've always loved the art of building a business. I went to college for business, and success stories fascinated me. So when I told Dad that I thought we needed to make changes to survive, he didn't exactly love the idea of focusing on just one product. He told me, "You'll never succeed just making end mills." We clashed for years over it, but one day, he started to see the issues we were facing and said, "You have bigger dreams than I have energy for. Maybe I should step aside and let you take over."

That's exactly what he did. Over the next five years, from 2002 to 2007, we transitioned the business, with Dad always watching from the sidelines—never too shy to tell me where I could improve. I valued his guidance, as well as that of my mom. They weren't just incredible parents; they were savvy business owners too.

A few years later, our business expanded into five countries. I was published in a national industrial magazine, and I received the national STEP Ahead Award in Washington, DC. Dad was proud, joking, "If I ever try to tell you how to run your business again, you should probably tell me to shut up."

Of course, building the business wasn't all sunshine and rainbows. Ownership of a small business is one of the toughest things you can take on. There were countless times when Rob and I questioned whether we'd survive. We purchased the business in 2007, only to face the crash of 2008. We had the same struggles finding skilled help that my dad had dealt with. There were days we wondered if we'd be better off working for someone else.

But as grueling and heartbreaking as it was, it was equally rewarding. Every obstacle we overcame and every challenge we met made the journey worth it.

In 2003, I founded ALS of Utica, a nonprofit that has raised over a million dollars to support countless families battling amyotrophic lateral sclerosis (ALS) in our community. The motivation behind this initiative runs deep. In 1999, just a year after we welcomed our first son, Michael, Rob's mom received the devastating diagnosis of ALS.

It was the cruelest disease I've ever witnessed, tearing through our family and turning our lives upside down.

During that harrowing time, I feared we wouldn't make it. Rob had to step away from our family, our business, and me to care for his mom. ALS leaves its victims completely dependent on others, requiring around-the-clock care for the most basic needs. I watched helplessly as my vibrant mother-in-law transformed into a wheelchair-bound shadow of herself, unable to move or speak.

You would have to have known Carolyn to grasp how shocking this change was. She was a whirlwind of energy—funny, outgoing, impeccably dressed, and full of life. She lit up every room she entered, paying attention to every detail. I'll never forget that one afternoon we found ourselves alone in her house after her diagnosis. The moment she broke down and cried struck me to my core. It was heartbreaking to witness her emotional pain. She knew she was dying, and the fear was palpable. She mourned the life she wouldn't get to see, the moments she would miss with her children.

That day left a profound impact on me, especially because Carolyn began shutting everyone out after her diagnosis. She didn't want anyone to see her suffering—not even her best friend. But that day, she allowed me to glimpse the depths of her soul, and I felt her pain in a way I never expected. She was a scared mother, powerless against what was happening to her. I know now that spending that day with her was what inspired me to honor her struggle, ultimately leading me to establish ALS of Utica in her memory.

What we endured never left me. ALS is a monster that makes you feel like you're drowning, gasping for air. I remember confiding in my mom about my struggles as a new mother to a colicky baby while Rob was away caring for his mom. I felt abandoned and longed for my husband's support.

My mom offered me the best advice I could have hoped for: "Find a way to cope without making Rob feel guilty. Let him do what he needs to for his mom, or he might resent you forever. Carolyn is dying, and time is limited. Let him be with her." She promised to help however she could, encouraged me to seek counseling if necessary, and reminded me that Rob needed the freedom to care for his mom.

My mom knew what she was talking about; she had taken care of her mother in her final days. She understood the difficulty of being torn in two directions and recognized that those last moments of life would mean everything to Rob.

Carolyn lived only four months after her diagnosis, enduring a brutal and swift decline. But when you're caught in the chaos of daily life, it's hard to know how to put one foot in front of the other. Each day can feel like an eternity, and you're unsure how long you can bear the weight of it all.

It often felt as though no one was there to help us. We received bits of advice here and there, but it wasn't nearly enough. The emotional toll was relentless. I yearned for someone who truly understood what we were facing. That's when ALS of Utica's mission began to take shape. We didn't just raise money to support families; we became their emotional lifeline, offering hope and assurance that even in the darkest moments, they would survive. I believed if we took care of the families, they would be better equipped to care for their loved ones.

I never intended for ALS of Utica to become as successful as it did. I always felt that God had a much larger plan for the organization than I could ever conceive. My work with patients and their families felt like a calling, a purpose that extended beyond myself. It was incredibly fulfilling to know that we were making a difference during their most desperate times. Helping them navigate their challenges never felt like work to me; rather, it was a privilege to be part of their lives during such dark hours. I forged lasting bonds with many of these families, and many of them are still our dear friends.

There's a special, unique joy that comes from making a difference in someone else's life. When you expect nothing in return for helping another human being in pain, you experience a joy that I believe God reserves as a special gift. Leading ALS of Utica has been one of the most fulfilling aspects of my life. The organization has thrived for over 20 years as an all-volunteer effort; no one has ever taken a dime in pay. It's a true labor of love. Our manufacturing business has covered most expenses, ensuring that every dollar we raise goes directly to the families who need it.

As much as I've given to these families, they have enriched my life in ways I never anticipated. They keep me grounded. Whenever I face a challenging day or feel that the world is closing in on me, a call from a family that's battling an ALS diagnosis quickly reminds me that my struggles pale in comparison to theirs.

Alongside managing Advanced Tool Inc. and ALS of Utica, I also found my calling as a business consultant. When people ask what I would do if money was no object, my answer is simple: I love helping small business owners navigate the challenges I've already faced. Although it comes naturally to me now, I remember and appreciate the struggle.

Ironically, I sometimes found I was better at assisting others with their businesses than running my own. Perhaps it was because the stakes felt lower when it wasn't my livelihood on the line. Solutions seemed clearer from the outside, away from the panic that enveloped me in my entrepreneurial journey.

Running a business is hard, plain and simple. I never truly felt content, for there are always issues to contend with. Each morning, I would try to count my blessings and feel gratitude; but to be honest, it was often a struggle. The only time I found genuine peace and contentment was when I was sitting on a beach, away from it all. It was there that I felt closest to God, able to pause and reflect on my life and all He had done for me.

If only I could have learned to pause and appreciate everything I had already achieved! I remember sitting in the grand event center in Washington, DC, waiting for my name to be called for a national award. A friend texted me, praising how monumental and amazing this moment was and asking how proud I felt. But at that moment, I realized I was already moving on to the next thing. It was as though I were on "autopilot," believing that stopping to savor success signaled weakness. I had to keep moving or risk being left behind.

Looking back, I see how sad that mindset was. Being an overachiever can feel like an affliction. I'm not sure I ever experienced happiness for an extended period. Most days were filled with feelings of being overwhelmed or a sense of failure. Although others perceived me as composed, happy, and confident, inside I felt anything but that. I was blind to the emptiness within me until God opened my eyes. Only then did I grasp the depth of what I had been missing.

The confidence I projected was hard earned, a reflection of the countless hours I poured into my work. Although I achieved much, I often didn't feel successful inside. My blood, sweat, and tears were woven into the very fabric of my journey. As a woman in a male-dominated industry, I navigated a landscape where few women dared to tread. I was there during a time when manufacturing was predominantly male, fighting through the glass ceiling while never stopping to acknowledge the pain and hurt inflicted by men who resented my presence just because I was female.

These men held power in their companies and could undermine my efforts with a snap of their fingers. In an instant, years of hard work and relationships I had cultivated could be obliterated, leaving me to scramble to find my footing again. I tried to avoid wallowing in self-pity; I told myself I had to regroup and move on without feeling the wounds. But deep down, that pain lingered. Ignoring it didn't make it disappear.

I believe this struggle contributed to my aversion to working in a sales role. I never grew a skin thick enough to endure the sting of rejection. When people said no to me, it felt personal. I have immense respect for salespeople; their profession is undoubtedly one of the toughest.

Despite the challenges, I aimed to be unstoppable. If one door closed, I sought out the next biggest opportunity and devised a way to work with that company instead. It became a thrilling challenge, a game to conquer. Securing a sale felt exhilarating, but even in victory, that high faded all too quickly. It was like chasing a fleeting rush, always craving the next fix.

I rarely felt satisfied—not just in business but in every aspect of my life. No achievement ever seemed good enough. The Bible warns of these traps, but I never paid any attention.

> *Everyone's toil is for their mouth, yet their appetite is never satisfied.* Ecclesiastes 6:7

Whoever loves money never has enough; whoever loves wealth is never satisfied with their income. This too is meaningless. Ecclesiastes 5:10

I always had a to-do list—constantly adding more tasks before I even had time to celebrate crossing things off. I thought this was a strength, a sign of ambition. Now I see it for what it was: exhausting. If I had even a spare minute, I'd scramble to fill it. I likely took on more than many might attempt, but as a small-business owner competing with large companies and their full teams, I often felt like I had to work as hard as ten people just to keep up. I wore the title "overachiever" like a badge of honor, convinced it was the only way to succeed.

But there were never enough hours in the day. The work was never done. I ran myself ragged, often skipping breaks and working through lunch, convinced that every moment spent resting was a missed opportunity to get ahead. I thought this relentless drive was a mark of a great work ethic.

It wasn't. It was a disease.

This grind came with costs. I spent so much energy striving for success during the day—checking off just one more item from that list—that by the time I got home, there was little left to give my husband and children. What I didn't realize then was that these would become my deepest regrets.

I wasn't just working hard; I was also obsessed with self-improvement. I took more courses than I can count, always on a quest to feel satisfied with myself. I was endlessly curious and eager to learn. If I didn't know how to do something, I'd figure it out. I'd watch a video, read a book, or find the best person in the field and learn from him or her. If the expert offered a program, I'd sign up. Being a college dropout made me feel as though I had something to prove, so I never stopped learning. I believed that being a lifelong learner was the secret to success.

My wall is lined with certificates and credentials. I've been trained by world-renowned leaders and spent thousands of dollars and countless hours trying to be the best version of myself, chasing some elusive definition of success. But I've come to realize that what I was chasing wasn't success. It was peace.

I always thought I'd finally feel content if I could finish that one last thing. I didn't see that I was trapped in an endless cycle, constantly moving the goalpost. Every new project seemed like *the* answer, the key to feeling whole. But it was never enough. I was on a hamster wheel, running harder but never getting anywhere.

Yes, I grew as a person, learned new skills, and felt more confident. But the deep, gnawing feeling that I wasn't enough never went away.

I lived this way for decades. Then, during COVID, something inside me shifted. My goals, my desires—they started to change. It was as if the constant striving began to lose its grip on me, and I started to see things differently.

Chapter Two
The Bible's Power

In 2020, the world felt like it was spinning out of control as we all tried to navigate the chaos of the COVID-19 pandemic. It was an awful, terrifying time. The news made it seem like everything around us was a potential death sentence—groceries, family, neighbors. The 24-hour news cycle fed us constant updates, with a relentless ticker counting every death and hospitalization.

I got swept up in the fear. I was scrubbing and disinfecting groceries before bringing them into the house. I'd take my clothes off at the door, trying to keep the virus out of my home. I followed the arrows in the grocery store, walking in one direction, wearing my mask as though it were armor. But deep down, nothing about it felt right. Everything in me screamed that this was all wrong. Still, the rule follower in me figured it was better to be safe than sorry.

Our business didn't shut down completely since we were considered "essential." But a big chunk of our income vanished overnight. We cut our hours in half, and I had no idea how we were going to survive financially. Still, my priorities had suddenly shifted from finances to the protection of my family.

In the middle of all that uncertainty, I found myself praying more. I realized the problem was bigger than anything I could handle myself. It was too big; I felt utterly unable to handle it solo. I needed God. Looking back, I see how limited my view of Him was. I thought of Him as the Big Boss you bother only when things are out of control, not for the everyday struggles.

I couldn't have been more wrong.

Fear gripped me, and I couldn't find comfort anywhere—not in the news, not in the world around me. So, I turned to the Bible. I had tried reading it before but found it impossible to understand. It was like reading another language. I'd start at the beginning, like any other book, but would give up before I got far. I didn't know that the Bible wasn't meant to be read like any other book. No one had ever told me about its power or how one sentence can say so much more than we realize.

I always felt a pull to read it, to know what God had to say, but part of me wondered why He didn't make it easier to understand.

At some point, someone recommended starting with the New Testament, specifically one of the shorter books. I think it was Paul Tripp, whose app I had started using. His five-minute videos introducing each book of the Bible were a game changer. He'd explain the background and give a summary, which made things start to click for me. So, I began with Ephesians, and for the first time, I was excited about understanding some of what I was reading.

What started as a simple goal to get more familiar with the Bible turned into a habit that changed my life. It took two and a half years, but I read the entire thing. I started with Ephesians, read all the way through Revelation, then went back to Matthew and worked my way to Galatians. When I finished the New Testament, I moved on to the Old Testament. It was harder to get through at first, but it quickly became one of my favorite parts.

Did I understand every single thing? Absolutely not! Sometimes I'd zone out or get lost in the long lists of unpronounceable names. I'd listen to the audio version while following along, but even that didn't always help. My mind would wander. It wasn't perfect, but the discipline of sticking with it transformed me.

I became invested not just in reading the Bible but also in understanding what God wanted me to know. I thought if I could get the Word of God inside of me, maybe it would start making more sense. Studying the Bible became my goal, and that's when things began to shift in my life. I'd love to say that simply picking up the Bible changed everything for me miraculously, but it wasn't that straightforward. What happened was much harder, yet more powerful: I started confronting the ugliness within myself that I didn't even know existed.

I had no idea that God's Word held the golden key to everything.

Before that, I rarely believed I was wrong. I was blind to my shortcomings and thought the rest of the world was the problem. If I messed up, it was because someone else forced my hand. I felt I was always just reacting, protecting myself from the mistakes of others.

When I hurt someone, I apologized—I didn't enjoy making those I loved feel bad. I tried to live by the Golden Rule: "Do unto others as you would have them do unto you." I truly believed this made me "good" because I did what was "right." I gave to charity, volunteered my time, and helped people in need. Heck, I even started an all-volunteer nonprofit that supported families suffering from ALS. People praised me for my work, and I honestly thought I had a guaranteed spot in Heaven, that my "good person" card was secure.

I had no idea how backward my thinking was.

God doesn't ask us to earn His love, but no one had ever told me that, or maybe I just wasn't listening. I didn't realize that trying to be "good enough" was the opposite of how God wants us to live. In fact, no amount of work, discipline, or moral behavior can earn salvation. We are saved by faith, not by deeds. This was so foreign to me. I was used to climbing mountains and conquering challenges. Accepting that I couldn't just try harder was difficult for me to comprehend. I thought I could "good person" my way into Heaven like the best of them. I didn't realize this mindset was a sin—a deadly one. It was pride.

"Why do you call me good?" Jesus answered. "No one is good—except God alone." Mark 10:18

13

The world applauded me for being an overachiever who could push through any obstacle, but that very drive kept me from getting closer to God.

The Bible is an extraordinary book. Slowly and gently, God's Word started to reveal things in me that I didn't know were there, things that had been blocking me from the peace and joy my heart craved.

Looking back, I'm still amazed at how much junk I had hidden from myself. It blows my mind how blind I was to *my* flaws. I had no idea how the darkness I couldn't see was affecting my life. But the Bible is like a miracle antidote—it takes the blinders off, layer by layer.

> *And immediately something like scales fell from his eyes,*
> *and he regained his sight....* Acts 9:18 ESV

At first, it's subtle, but eventually, it digs deep enough to reveal a person you don't even recognize.

I could never have imagined that the greatest gift of my life would come from being brave enough to face the ugliness in me. I hadn't realized what I was keeping hidden—not only from others, but also from myself. As I drew closer to God's light, I began to see parts of myself I hadn't noticed before.

It's like living with a rotten tooth. On the outside, it might look fine, but underneath, it's infected, spreading poison to everything around it. We might be too afraid to deal with it, worried about what we'll look like if it's gone. But when we finally get brave enough to pull it, the relief is incredible. We wonder why we didn't take care of it sooner. Sin is the same way—it hides deep within us, even from ourselves.

I never realized how much I was battling pride.

I remember coming across a meme that said, "The problem is, I expect *me* out of people." I thought, *Yes, exactly!* It felt so validating. I didn't see anything wrong with wishing people would think or act like I did. After all, how many times do we ask, "What is wrong with people?" It seemed normal, especially when so many others felt the same way.

But here's a truth that is hard for me to admit: I often thought people were lazy. I thought they didn't achieve as much because they didn't work as hard. I didn't realize how dangerous and ugly that mindset was. It was rooted in judgment.

I've since learned that confidence isn't always a virtue. It can become a slippery slope. I used to wish others around me would try harder to be as resourceful or driven as I was. Looking back, I'm not sure when I developed such a sense of self-assurance. As a teenager, I had no confidence at all. Maybe I was overcompensating for those feelings of inferiority.

In business meetings, surrounded by other owners, we'd all complain about the same thing: how we could be more successful if we could just find employees who were more like us. This mindset was common, but it only fed my pride. And it didn't stop at work.

At home, I'd get frustrated when my family didn't load the dishwasher *my* way or when they put things in the "wrong" place. I'd think, *Why can't they see this is the better way to do it?* I was so judgmental; I would thank God for making me more resourceful and what I thought was *better* than others. Imagine that!

I cringe looking back; I can see how completely deluded I was. I was thanking God for the very sin He wanted to expose and remove from my life. I had no idea how tightly the enemy had gripped me in my self-righteousness.

God's Word warns us about this exact thing—of thinking too highly of ourselves.

> *The Pharisee stood by himself and prayed: "God, I thank you that I am not like other people—robbers, evildoers, adulterers—or even like this tax collector."* Luke 18:11

> *I tell you that this man, rather than the other, went home justified before God. For all those who exalt themselves will be humbled, and those who humble themselves will be exalted.* Luke 18:14

I had a problem, and I was reluctant to admit it. I learned that pride is self-worship, not recognizing that all the goodness in me came from a source much greater than myself. It finally clicked that my talents and strengths weren't the result of my years of effort and learning, as I had always believed. Instead, I realized that any success I achieved was due to the gifts and abilities that God had placed within me. My hard work and education, while important, didn't create my achievements; they were merely a response to the potential He had already instilled in me. The truth is, God could take it all away in an instant, and there were times in my life when He did just that.

> *To this John replied, "A person can receive only what is given them from heaven."* John 3:27

Looking back, I can see that every time life pulled the rug out from under me, it wasn't bad luck. It was God ensuring I stayed on the right path. My husband and I often complained that for every step forward we took in business, it felt like we were taking two steps back. We could never seem to get ahead. But now I realize that those setbacks were God's way of protecting me or working on my character. They were His guardrails, gently nudging me back when I started to feel too self-sufficient.

Whenever I thought, *I've got this, God; I can handle it from here,* something crushing would inevitably bring me back to my knees, reminding me of my need for His help. That was His design all along—to protect me from myself. And for that, I am profoundly grateful. Everything I was chasing was never going to give me the peace I have now.

If only I could tell my younger self to stop fighting against the currents when things didn't go my way. I'd reassure her that God was at work, orchestrating a master plan superior to anything she could imagine. I was blind to it all—I didn't know what I didn't know—and that blindness was not overcome permanently at that time. But once you awaken to the secret of life and experience His joy and peace, you can't help but want to share it with the world. Life is undeniably sweeter when we step aside and let Him take the lead.

I love the analogy of a parent and a toddler. Think about how often we swoop in to rescue our children before they can get hurt. They might be joyfully climbing a bookshelf to reach the toy on top, completely unaware that the shelf is about to topple over. We rush in, only to be met with their tears of frustration as they don't understand that we just saved them from disaster.

In this analogy, God is the loving parent, and we adults, thinking we have everything figured out, are just toddlers blissfully unaware of the dangers He's protecting us from.

The Bible warns us that pride is a sin that leads to destruction. I used to think only the arrogant and obnoxious struggled with that. But to my surprise, I discovered it lurking within me in abundance. It's a struggle we all face.

> *Pride goes before destruction, a haughty spirit before a fall.* Proverbs 16:18

***

In January 2024, I was devastated after losing a major business account, feeling the weight of worry for my future pressing down on me. Seeking comfort, I turned to my friend Robin, one of my Bible study leaders, and shared my heartache with her. As we talked, I hoped for words of encouragement to lift my spirits.

She listened intently and asked insightful questions, and I waited for her gentle words to soothe my hurt. But then she suggested I check out Tim Keller's "The Evil of Envy" podcast. *Wait, what?* I thought, confused. I needed a discussion about fear or anxiety, not envy. Everything inside me told me she must not understand, she's missing the point. Yet, Robin was a woman of God, and I respected her wisdom. Despite my doubts, I decided to give the podcast a listen.

Oh my goodness! That podcast hit me like a ton of bricks. Tim Keller explained that envy is a deadly sin that can drain our joy as nothing else can. He urged us to examine our deepest desires and reflect on how we feel when someone else has what we long for. Are we truly happy at that person's success? Or does a twinge of resentment lurk beneath the surface?

That question struck a chord. I wasn't celebrating my competitor's win—not at all. I wanted that business, and I was grappling with resentment over it. I questioned, *Isn't it okay, though?* It's just business. Business is competitive, after all. I thought it was normal to want what my competitors had and to chase after it. I didn't think this could have been what God meant by coveting. Winning at all costs was the name of the game, right?

But now, listening to Tim Keller's words, I began to see a side of myself—another ugly side—that I hadn't acknowledged. I craved money and success; I wanted to dominate my competition. But if I viewed them as real people, then my feelings of jealousy started to seem far more sinister.

The Bible teaches that a godly person rejoices in others' success.

> *Rejoice with those who rejoice; mourn with those who mourn.* Romans 12:15

But does that include when they have the very thing we want more than anything? Was rejoicing at that point even possible? *I* didn't feel that way. Tim Keller pointed out that envy is something none of us wants to admit to because it forces us to confront our pettiness. He warned that envy often lurks in the shadows of our lives unnoticed.

It took weeks of wrestling with this idea before I could accept that I was battling envy. I think we all do. Those feelings might appear harmless, but they are anything but.

We see "Kate," who seems to glide effortlessly through life with endless vacation time, and we wish our jobs were as easy as hers. Then there's good-looking "Mark," who can eat whatever he likes without gaining an ounce, and "Jack and Sue," whose seemingly perfect marriage and idyllic life leave us feeling inadequate. We tell ourselves these are just observations, but deep down, we know they tap into something more profound within us.

But here's a telling way to gauge whether we're wrestling with an ugly demon of envy. How would we feel if Kate's company started requiring a much harder work schedule? Would a small part of us secretly breathe a sigh of relief, thinking, *At least I'm not alone in my struggles*? Does life feel more balanced when we see someone else face the same setbacks we face?

What about Mark—would we feel a flicker of satisfaction if he suddenly sprouted a massive pimple on that perfect face of his? Or when we learn that Jack and Sue's seemingly flawless marriage isn't so perfect after all, do we feel a pang of empathy—but also a little comfort knowing their relationship also has flaws? Certainly, we don't want to see others in pain, but does that realization make us feel just a bit better about our own less-than-ideal lives?

Consider the world of Hollywood, filled with its glamorous, rich, and stunningly perfect celebrities. Tabloid magazines thrive and negative posts go viral for a reason; seeing those at the pinnacle of success stumble can give us a strange sense of relief, as if they're being pulled down closer to our level.

Why does someone else's misfortune seem to lighten our burdens? I guess it's true what they say: "Misery loves company." Yet, we often don't label these feelings as envy; we just chalk it up to everyday life. But the Bible offers a cautionary warning about envy, urging us to reflect on the hidden emotions that can creep into our hearts.

A heart at peace gives life to the body, but envy rots the bones. Proverbs 14:30

Envy can quietly consume us and poison our ability to enjoy the life we have by pushing us to compare ourselves to others. There's always someone with more money, a better career, or a seemingly perfect marriage, and this comparison makes it easy to feel as though what we have will never be enough. But what happens when we look in the mirror and realize we don't like who we've become?

That's when we turn to God. Only He can free us from the grip of envy and the compulsion to keep up with those around us. Surrendering to Him was the only way I could break free. God challenged me to face my truth. I began writing down everything I was jealous of—everything I thought I needed to be happy. I wanted wealth so I wouldn't have to work another day in my life. I envied the man in Florida with the yacht and beachfront home. I was jealous of couples whose marriages seemed flawless when mine wasn't.

At first, the Bible's talk of idols confused me. To me, idols were ancient gods that people worshipped. How could something like wealth or a yacht be an idol? I didn't *worship* them; I just *wanted* them! That's normal, right? Everyone needs money to survive. I couldn't live in poverty. I kept justifying my desires, not realizing that the things I was clinging to were standing in the way of the life God had planned for me. What He had in store was far better than anything I could have dreamed of.

The more I read the Bible, the clearer it became. God wants us to love *Him*, not material things. My days were spent chasing money, success, and status. But God? I barely thought of Him unless something went wrong or I needed His comfort. It hit me that no matter how much I achieved, nothing was ever good enough—it couldn't ever fill the emptiness I felt. Relationships, beauty, and success would always come up short. It made sense—if God created a space inside of us that only He can fill, then nothing else will ever satisfy. Not a yacht. Not wealth. Not status.

Walking through these new realizations wasn't easy, especially when I admitted that maybe Robin had been right all along. I finally understood why God stresses the importance of community with other believers. They help us see the things we can't see in ourselves.

The strange thing is, after confronting my envy, the pain I felt over a lost business account started to fade. Some might call it denial, but it wasn't. Nothing had changed—the account was still gone. But I felt a peace that didn't make sense. It was as if God was showing me that His way of living was so much better than mine. I liked the peace I was finding, and it made me eager to ask God to reveal even more things that didn't belong in my heart.

> *And the peace of God, which surpasses all understanding, will guard your hearts and your minds in Christ Jesus.* Philippians 4:7 ESV

Once I mustered the courage to face my flaws, it was as though a floodgate opened, bringing so much more into the light. I realized I had been holding onto years of unforgiveness toward others and even toward my husband. And there was shame too—shame I hadn't wanted to acknowledge. Slowly, I began to understand that maybe the Bible was right all along. Maybe we are all, at our core, deeply flawed.

> *The Lord saw how great the wickedness of the human race had become on the earth, and that every inclination of the thoughts of the human heart was only evil all the time.* Genesis 6:5

Chapter Three
Going Deeper

I was raised Catholic, and my relationship with the church ebbed and flowed over the years. There were times when going to Mass felt important, a way to connect with God. But there were also long stretches when I didn't feel I needed it or got much from it at all. I'd sit in the pew more out of guilt or the vague hope that maybe, just maybe, showing up would put me in good standing with God. I wanted Him in my corner, especially when things got tough. I guess I thought being present in church was enough to make God happy with me.

When I hit my 30s in the 2000s and had children, life became more complicated. My marriage was harder than I'd expected, and I found myself seeking God more than I ever had before. But even though I kept going to church, I still felt empty. That's when I started watching TV preachers. They spoke in ways that made sense to me— open, real, and unafraid to admit *their* flaws. It was different from the Catholic upbringing I'd known, where the focus felt more on rituals than on the messiness of life. These preachers helped me open the Bible for the first time and grasp what the Scriptures were saying.

Dr. Charles Stanley was one of my favorites. His messages stirred something in me—they made me want to know God better, to live more in line with His Word. Even though I had grown up Catholic and gone through all the sacraments, I hadn't truly given my heart to Christ. That journey started one morning when I said a prayer of salvation in front of my TV while Dr. Stanley was on: "Lord, I'm a sinner; I repent of my sins. I believe in Jesus, that He took the punishment for my sins, died, and rose again. I give my heart to You, Lord."

From that moment on, I considered myself a saved believer, on the path to Heaven. For nearly 20 years, TV became my church. I prayed regularly and believed I had a solid relationship with God. I knew He loved me, and I believed He wanted me to be happy. And I was grateful to know He was there, especially during life's darkest moments—like when my grandfather passed away, my mother-in-law was diagnosed with ALS, and my sisters battled cancer. God was my anchor through it all.

But it's only now, looking back, that I realize how one-sided my relationship with Him was. I thought I was giving God everything, but I wasn't. I was holding back parts of my heart and life, and I didn't know it. I believed God's only desire was for me to be happy, so I never saw my attachment to money, success, and enjoying life as a problem. I didn't realize I was missing something deeper—a true, wholehearted surrender to Him. It took time, but eventually, I began to see that God wanted so much more from me than I'd been willing to give.

If I had known that living outside of God's ways was holding me back from His greatest blessings, I might have set different goals. I had no idea that the way I was living was wrong, making life far more difficult than it needed to be. If someone had told me about the overwhelming peace, love, and joy that come from surrendering to God, maybe I would've been willing to give Him my whole heart a lot sooner.

I wish someone had shaken me and made me see what I was missing. Maybe wiser people tried, but I didn't listen. I was stubborn, convinced I knew better. Looking back now, I realize that so many of the struggles I faced were self-inflicted, brought on by my pride and insistence on doing everything my way. Life didn't have to be that hard, but I was determined to be independent.

I once heard a preacher say that you can go to church every week and still not be saved. You can hear the Word of God without ever letting it sink deep enough into your heart to change it. That was me for much of my life. I justified things I knew didn't align with "being saved" because I had convinced myself that God was only loving and He'd be okay with it.

I had no concept of what real sin was. As a Catholic, I knew how to confess what I thought were sins to a priest—lying to my mom, fighting with my sister, sometimes even making things up just to have something to confess. But I was completely blind to the real darkness in my heart. I didn't know how much ugliness was buried inside.

It didn't help that I looked down on people I thought were "too holy." I saw "Bible thumpers" and "Jesus freaks" as people who were outwardly so godly that they couldn't possibly be having any fun. I avoided church services that went too long. Too much worship music annoyed me. My heart wasn't in it. I wasn't there to worship God—I was there to check off a box and feel like a "good girl." In my mind, church was my ticket to not going to hell.

I didn't understand the concept of "works." I wish I had read the Bible sooner, because then I would've learned that there's nothing we can do to earn our way to God. It's not about doing things; no amount of effort will ever be enough.

For someone like me—who's spent life doing, achieving, pushing to be the best—the idea that all God asks of me is to believe in Jesus was hard to wrap my head around. Its simplicity baffled me. How could something so important not require more from me? It took me years to finally grasp that salvation isn't about what I do—it's about who He is.

> *For by grace you have been saved through faith. And this is not your own doing; it is the gift of God, not a result of works, so that no one may boast.* Ephesians 2:8–9 ESV

> *But if it is by grace, it is no longer on the basis of works; otherwise grace would no longer be grace.* Romans 11:6 ESV

One of my biggest blind spots was that I didn't truly believe in Satan—or realize that many things I loved were in reality his tools. I had no idea how easily I could be deceived, but now I see how completely I fell for his schemes.

The more I read the Bible, the clearer it became: the evil wasn't just "out there"—it was inside of me too. Without seeking God's help every day, I was more likely to find myself on Team Satan than Team Jesus. Once I caught a glimpse of how blind I had been, I became obsessed with discovering what else I didn't know. I had spent too much time believing nothing could get past me. I was shocked by the depths of my ignorance.

As I delved deeper into God's Word, I could feel my heart softening. I began to change—not by force, but naturally. Certain things I used to enjoy didn't appeal to me anymore. I didn't have to "work" so hard to live better. God was changing me from the inside out.

I became more patient. Not perfect, but calmer. I started to forgive more easily—mostly because I began to see *my* flaws more clearly and realized I wasn't so perfect after all. I loved people more and got annoyed less easily. Troubles that once overwhelmed me became manageable. Not every day was perfect, but there was a new strength inside me. I felt more joy and more peace, and for the first time in my life, I didn't feel the need to control everything. I was learning to surrender, trusting that God was in control and I didn't have to be. I had a greater hope for the future and a desire to see what God would do next.

My prayers weren't just something I rushed through to check off my to-do list anymore. They became my most sacred time—moments when I connected with God, reading His Word and learning new things. The Bible, which I once saw as a dry, old book, fascinated me. I couldn't get enough. The wisdom it held, the way it spoke to me no matter what was happening in my life—it was alive in a way I'd never experienced before.

I'm only beginning to understand how far into our hearts God can pour Himself. He's always ready to take us further, to show us more. My walk with Christ is no longer about hearing a good message on Sunday and going through the motions. I genuinely look forward to church now, and I cherish starting my mornings with God every day of the week.

Worship music used to drive me crazy; now it moves me to tears. It speaks to my soul, reminding me of Christ's sacrifice and the promise of what's to come. When life gets tough, now that music reminds me that God is right here, ready to hold me when I need to break down.

It took me over half of a century to reach this point in my relationship with God. Part of me wishes I'd learned this sooner, but I've come to see that God's timing is perfect. The road I traveled to get this close to Him wasn't easy, but maybe that's the point. We don't usually seek God when everything's going great. He lets trials draw us closer, to make us finally surrender.

For most of my life, I lived for God because I wanted to have my prayers answered and stand before Him when I die. I didn't realize that I didn't truly love Him. My motives were all wrong. But after immersing myself in the Bible, I've come to know God, and in knowing Him, I can't help but love Him completely.

The greatest lesson I've learned is that when we surrender our lives to God, we get a taste of eternal life on earth. My life became much sweeter, filled with joy and peace I had never known. This contentment I'd been chasing all my life—it was there, waiting for me in Him. I had to stop looking for it in all the wrong places.

Chapter Four
Looking Good

I spent most of my life worrying about what others thought of me and how I came across to them. I might have appeared confident, but underneath, I was always trying to feel "good enough"—trying to get the world to like me. In my career, I tried to stand out enough to be successful but not so much that I might offend someone if I went against the "norm."

My dad was the opposite. He always spoke his mind. On one hand, I admired his bravery, but on the other, I was embarrassed if he said something I thought might be confrontational, especially when it didn't seem to faze him. So instead, I spent my life trying to fit in with the world, trying to not rock the boat, and trying to please everyone. I became an expert at adapting to whoever was in the room and becoming who I thought those people wanted me to be, showing just enough of myself to be accepted. But honestly, I was so focused on pleasing others that at times I lost sight of my own identity.

But who was I really? Who was I when it was just me and God and I couldn't hide or pretend to be something I wasn't?

I never left the house without makeup, scared someone might see my bare face. Deep down, I didn't feel pretty enough to let others see the real me. One of the hardest moments of my life came when I was diagnosed with rosacea. My face broke out in red bumps, rashes, and pimples that no amount of makeup could cover. It was my worst nightmare. I cried almost every day, staring into the mirror, trying to hide what couldn't be hidden.

Ironically, it was 2020, and masks became my saving grace. Although I doubted their ability to stop the spread of COVID-19, I was relieved to wear one because it hid my rosacea.

When my doctor told me rosacea was incurable, something inside me knew he was wrong. He said I'd need low-dose antibiotics and steroids for life. But after working with ALS patients for 20 years—some of who defied the odds their doctors gave them—I believed I could do the same. I embarked on a journey to heal myself. I became a certified detox specialist and was determined to understand what causes disease and how to eliminate toxins from the body.

For a whole year, starting in 2019, I ate nothing but fruits, vegetables, and herbs. It was brutal. I'll never forget sitting at Thanksgiving dinner with a plate of watermelon while everyone else feasted on turkey and stuffing. My mouth watered, and it felt like torture, but I stuck with it.

In the end, it was worth every agonizing minute. My rosacea healed, and I never had to take any medication. I proved my doctor wrong and beat the odds, just as some of my ALS patients had taught me was possible. ALS patients are told there is nothing left for them, no surgeries, and less than a handful of drugs that might extend their lives by only a few months. They are told to go home, get their affairs in order, and prepare to die.

But I'll never forget Rachel, an ALS patient who ran a Facebook group for others like her. She told me something that stuck with me: "If you want to help ALS patients live, tell them to seek beyond their doctor's advice."

At first, I thought she was crazy. But then I started following other ALS patients, talking to them, and asking questions. I was amazed at what I found. These people weren't just going home and preparing to die like they were told; instead, they were outliving their diagnoses by years—sometimes living three, four, or five times longer than their doctors predicted. They were sharing everything they were trying in private groups, swapping tips on how to live beyond the limitations they'd been given.

They talked about avoiding medications that caused more harm than good, cutting out preservatives and pesticides, and sticking to organic, non-GMO foods. They pointed out that many of the chemicals banned in other countries are still allowed in the US, and that our everyday lives were overloading our bodies with toxins—from cleaning products to laundry detergent and even air fresheners. It was overwhelming, but how could I ignore the fact that these people, given death sentences, were the ones showing me how to live?

It turns out, they were right. My journey to healing from rosacea led me to realize that what we put in and on our bodies matters. Their bravery in questioning everything they were told helped me find the strength to do the same.

These people were dying. They had nothing to gain, nothing to sell. They were simply trying to help each other live. They'd share their before-and-after bloodwork, offering tangible proof of their progress. Thousands of people in these groups were fighting to live, sharing what worked and what didn't.

It was a revelation, especially since I'd never questioned my doctors before. I did everything they told me, trusting them completely. Then Rachel asked me a question that stopped me in my tracks: "Did you know the third leading cause of death in America is medical and physician error?" I had no idea.

Since 2015, five years before my rosacea diagnosis, I had been diving deep into research on ALS, reading PubMed articles and medical studies. I had started to believe that under the right circumstances, the human body could heal itself. I was even hearing about documented cases of ALS reversals. So, when I was diagnosed with rosacea and told it was incurable, I decided to take a different path. If all that my doctors could offer was a medication that wouldn't even solve the problem, what did I have to lose by trying something unconventional?

I made it my mission to remove everything in my life that might be causing an issue—starting with my food. I cut out dairy, sugar, and grains. I ate only organic fruits and vegetables. I scrutinized the ingredients in everything I used: lotions, shampoo, laundry detergent, dish soap. I weaned myself off every medication. If it didn't come from nature, I didn't want it near me. I figured the more toxins I removed, the better my chances of healing.

It wasn't easy. It took two years for my rosacea to disappear. The first year, I stuck to an almost entirely fruit-and-vegetable diet. By the second, I reintroduced carbs at dinner—oh, how I had missed them! After reading *The China Study*, I avoided meat and dairy for even longer. I also adopted intermittent fasting, having only fruit juice until noon, a smoothie in the afternoon, and dinner in the evening.

I know there's a lot of debate about fruit sugars, but based on all the studies I'd read, I trusted that sugar from fruit didn't require insulin the way other sugars did. And although I'm not a doctor, I can tell you what worked for me: my sugar levels were no longer out of normal range, and my bloodwork improved dramatically. Plus, I trusted the fruits God created—they felt healing to me.

That period of my life changed the way I viewed disease. It made me realize that what we put in and on our bodies has a much bigger impact on our health than we're led to believe. We fill ourselves with processed foods and alcohol and then wonder why our bodies rebel. Our skin is our largest organ, and I believe the illnesses we experience show up in the weakest areas of our bodies. For me, it was my skin.

Unfortunately, this wouldn't be the last time I'd have a skin issue. In February 2024, I went to Florida for a vacation with my husband. It was a week of eating out, multiple meals a day, with hot fudge sundaes at night.

By Wednesday of that week, I noticed that my eyelids were becoming irritated. I thought it was my seasonal allergies kicking in since the pollen count was high in the South. I didn't think much of it until I got back home.

A week later, there was snow on the ground, I was still having issues with my eyelids, and the problem was getting worse. My eyelids would swell up, turn beet red, and burn to the point where I had to put ice packs on them. I had no idea what was going on with my face.

It was easy to rule out seasonal allergies because it was February, and I was back home in New York with lots of cold and snow. Nothing was growing outside to flare up seasonal allergies.

I wondered if it could be a food reaction. Some of my bad eating habits from being on vacation lingered, so I went back to a super clean diet of mostly fruits and vegetables and seemed to do better. One night I walked into the house after work. Rob made pasta for dinner. I ate it, not thinking anything of it. The next morning, I woke up with terribly swollen and burning eyelids again. I thought, *You have got to be kidding me.* I started paying attention to what I had eaten before a flare-up, but it didn't make sense because one day my eyelids blew up after eating an orange.

I went to my doctor, and she told me to go on a carnivore diet. She said most people don't react negatively to meat, but she also wasn't convinced it was food allergies. She believed that, somehow, I must have come in contact with a toxin that overloaded my body and caused severe inflammation. She said that's why inflammatory foods such as sugar, gluten, and grains were sending my body over the edge.

The flare-up would last for three to four days. Once again, I was dealing with going out in public and looking hideous. Again, I was crying when I looked at myself in the mirror.

The carnivore diet did not work well for me. While on it, I did not feel good. Since I'd reacted to an orange, I was concerned about going back to a high-fruit diet.

A few people said it sounded as though I might be dealing with an autoimmune problem. This led me to the AIP diet (autoimmune protocol diet). You eliminate everything from your diet except for certain vegetables and some fruits and slowly incorporate other foods back into your diet until you figure out what your body can or can't handle.

I was miserable. My diet was so restrictive it was ridiculous, but my eyelids weren't flaring anymore. I was once again facing how much eating affected my life. I hadn't realized how much I loved eating until I couldn't. I forgot how much our lives revolved around food. I couldn't have family dinners anymore, go out to eat with my husband or girlfriends, or go anywhere with others for any length of time because I couldn't stop somewhere to eat.

I prayed. I begged God to make it go away. It had been three months, and I couldn't live like that. I wondered if the cause of my condition might be the stress of the business struggles we were facing. Maybe the cause was the stress over almost losing my dad a couple of months prior. He had a brain bleed and emergency brain surgery in Arizona. Doctors said it was a miracle he walked away relatively unscathed. I had been sick with the flu for the first three weeks in January, so maybe my body was still weak. Maybe I was exposed to something in Florida. Honestly, I had no idea.

I went to a functional medicine doctor next. She ordered nine vials of bloodwork, and they all came back normal. She was also concerned about possible toxic exposure. She suggested maybe my symptoms resulted from something in the room or around where I stayed in Florida. She said the AIP diet was smart and that I should stick to it. She said she understood how hard that was, for she had been on it herself.

Life was overwhelming. Not being able to eat hardly any food felt cruel. I had done well for three weeks on the AIP diet. Not one flare-up. But I had an upcoming wedding to attend, and I was super nervous about the dinner. I hoped I had given my body enough of a break so I'd be okay and get through one meal without a reaction. I didn't eat a lot, but unfortunately, I felt my eyes starting to swell before I went to bed that night. I was devastated.

Chapter Five
My Encounter

It took four days for my swollen eyelids to return to normal after the wedding dinner. By Sunday, May 5, 2024, I looked fine on the outside, but inside, I was a wreck. I was at my breaking point, consumed by one thought: *How am I supposed to keep living if I'm allergic to everything?* I couldn't understand why my body was betraying me like this. I was devastated.

During the church service that day, Pastor Michael Servello Jr. spoke about God's miraculous healing power. The moment those words left his mouth, it felt like they were meant just for me. It was as if God were speaking directly through him, offering me a sliver of hope that my health and food issues could be healed. I wanted so badly to believe that. I *needed* to believe it.

The sermon was about how life can be unbearably hard sometimes and how negative thoughts are often from the enemy, making things even worse. Pastor Mike shared stories of people in the Bible who felt trapped, as though the weight of the world were on their shoulders. I could relate.

He spoke about Saul and David, two kings who dealt with life's struggles very differently. Saul tried to handle everything on his own, never turning to God, relying only on his own strength and wisdom. I winced—I saw myself in that. I had always been someone who rarely asked for help.

David, on the other hand, lived a life devoted to the Lord. When trouble surrounded him, he fell to his knees and worshipped, no matter how foolish he looked to others. He didn't care. Even when his wife ridiculed him for his outward, passionate displays of worship, he stayed true to his faith. Hearing this, I suddenly felt ashamed of all the times I silently judged people in church for what I thought was "over-worshipping." I'd always assumed they were showing off, trying to seem like "better Christians" with their arms raised and emotional responses to the music. It never occurred to me that they might really be feeling God move in their hearts.

Then Pastor Mike paused and asked, "Can I ask you something? Who here is afraid to raise their hands in worship because they worry about how they'll look?"

Ouch. I felt a pang of conviction. God *was* working on me that day. I'd always thought hand-raisers looked silly. Growing up Catholic, I'd never seen that kind of thing before—it was foreign to me. My heart was softening toward them, but I wasn't ready to join them. Not yet, anyway.

Throughout the service, emotions bubbled up. When Pastor Mike asked, "Who needs chains broken off their life today? If that's you, step forward for prayer," I could barely hold back the tears. I felt those chains—around my health, my business, my entire life. It was too much. I felt trapped, overwhelmed, and broken.

A few people went up to the front. I wanted to—I felt God calling me—but I was frozen in place, too scared to move. Tears welled up in my eyes. Robin, sitting next to me, knew how much I'd been struggling. She turned toward me.

"You want to go up, don't you?"

I nodded. "Yes."

"Do you want me to go with you?"

"No. I'm going." I stood up and left my seat.

What happened next is a blur. I don't remember everything I said, but I do remember crying—really crying, as if decades of pain were finally being released. My shoulders shook as Amy, one of the ladies on the prayer team, prayed over me. I could feel God's presence right there with me, helping me let go of the burdens and chains I'd carried for so long.

When I returned to my seat, my eyes were still full of tears. I wasn't sure what I was feeling—relief, confusion, maybe a little fear. Robin could sense I was resisting something deep inside.

"Accept Him, Sherry. Just accept Him," she said softly. She grabbed my hands and began praying for me. I closed my eyes, and for the first time, I felt an overwhelming desire to surrender—to give my life to God. My way of living wasn't working anymore. The tight grip I had on trying to control everything was slipping, failing. As tears streamed down my face, I felt God moving into my heart, setting up a home. I was His now.

After that, everything felt different. Softer. Lighter. Humbled. God felt *so close*, like He was right there with me everywhere I went. I'd heard people talk about the hole inside us that only God can fill, but mine wasn't just filled—it was spilling over with His presence. Where had this feeling been my whole life?

A thought crossed my mind—was my food allergy healed? I was scared to hope.

The next day, Monday, I was still basking in God's presence. I reflected on something I had journaled earlier that week, a prayer request I'd shared at Bible study. It stopped me in my tracks. My requests were always about family, work, or health—prayers for the things that were weighing on me. But this time, my prayer was simple: "to hear from God." I didn't even remember writing that. And then it hit me—God had not only heard me, He'd answered me in a way I could never have imagined. He let me feel Him in the clearest, most powerful way possible.

I'd never felt so full of the Lord, so at peace.

On Tuesday morning, I sat outside for my prayer time. The sun was shining, a perfect May morning. But as I reflected on everything that had happened, I was hit with a wave of sadness—sadness over how I had lived up until that point, keeping God at arm's length for so many years. I had been running on empty for so long, I didn't even realize there was another way to live. For the first time, I truly grasped the weight of my choices and how they had affected my life, my business, my marriage.

I didn't think I had any tears left, but they came, streaming down my face. I felt broken, overwhelmed by the world's darkness and my own failures. I didn't have the answers, and for the first time, I wasn't pretending that I did. I began to sob.

And in that raw, vulnerable moment, God's presence surrounded me. *I felt Him.* It was as if He wrapped me in His arms, holding me close as I cried. I was in a cocoon, sheltered under His wings. For the first time in my life, I felt God's presence and knew I wasn't alone.

> *He will cover you with his feathers, and under his wings*
> *you will find refuge....* Psalm 91:4

The more I felt His presence, the more the tears flowed. It was like years of pain and frustration were being released all at once. I could feel the chains that had held me down for so long breaking off, one by one.

But then, something extraordinary happened—something beyond anything I could have ever imagined.

I don't know how long I had been crying, but when I finally looked up, I saw something in front of me. Directly across from me, there was a faint, transparent silhouette—a shape that seemed larger than life, almost like a mountain. I don't have the words to describe it, but I knew it was the Lord. He had comforted me through my tears, and now He was sitting right there with me.

I felt so unworthy, so overwhelmed. I broke down again, crying even harder, and said out loud, "I'm not worthy of this. I'm not worthy of being in Your presence."

I couldn't believe what was happening, but at the same time, I had no doubt who was before me. Still, I asked, "Why would You sit with me? Don't You have way more important things to do?"

In my spirit, I heard Him say, "There is nowhere else I'd rather be."

And I lost it. I sobbed uncontrollably, overcome by a love so pure and so powerful, I couldn't even grasp it. The thought kept running through my mind, *Me? Really? The* Lord *wants to sit with* me? It was the most beautiful, sacred moment I had ever experienced.

I began pouring out my heart, just talking to God, having a conversation with Him. I didn't hear an audible voice, but I could feel His responses in my spirit. Here's how that conversation went.

I said, "Lord, I've screwed up. I thought I knew what to do; I thought I knew everything. But I don't even know who I am anymore, or what I'm supposed to be doing."

His answer was simple: "Perfect."

I confessed, "I've hurt my marriage, and I've been horrible to Rob."

He was silent, but His presence stayed with me, unwavering.

I continued, "I'm scared of all the evil in the world. It feels like everything is trying to hurt us."

He replied, "Reread everything you highlighted in your Bible today."

I had been reading Isaiah 26, and when I looked back, I saw that I had highlighted passages about God destroying the wicked and punishing the evil in the world.

I told Him, "I'm sorry that I've made food an idol in my life. I'm so scared about my health and these food problems."

And He said, "You are healed."

Then I asked, "Can I just sit here with You?"

His answer? "Yes."

I felt an overwhelming peace, but I also wanted to write it all down. I didn't want to forget a single moment of what was happening. So, I asked Him if it was okay to write, and I felt His patience as I jotted everything down.

I had one more concern.

"If I tell anyone about this, they'll think I'm crazy."

He simply said, "Tell them anyway."

We sat together in silence for a while longer. Then He told me it wasn't my job to worry about punishing evil—that was His job. My job was to love and to live in peace with everyone.

I was in complete awe. I didn't want to leave His presence. I didn't want to move. I was 45 minutes late to work that day, but I didn't care. It was the most peaceful, beautiful experience of my life.

When I finally stood up and went inside, my body was trembling. I wasn't cold, but I was shaking as if I were freezing. I felt nervous, excited, peaceful, and even a little skeptical, all at once. I kept thinking, *Did that really happen? Did I imagine the whole thing?*

But deep down, I knew without a doubt that the Lord had sat with me—and that I was forever changed.

Chapter Six
Proof

That day in May wasn't the first time I had heard God speak to me. I had been hearing from Him for years, so when that encounter in my backyard happened, His voice was already familiar to me.

How do I know it's God and not just my own thoughts? Because He often says things I don't want to hear. One of the easiest ways I've found to hear Him is through journaling. During my morning prayer time, I pour my heart onto the pages. It helps me quiet the noise, clear the stress, and open myself up to His guidance. I ask Him for help and for direction, or sometimes I just ask, "What do You want me to know today?" Then I write whatever He places on my heart.

The first time I realized it was truly God speaking, I was complaining about Rob. I was praying—more like venting—and asking God to change him. I listed all the ways I thought Rob was wrong, point by point, laying it all out in my journal. I asked God to fix him.

But the response I got? It wasn't what I expected. I started writing down all the things *I* needed to change. "Wait, what? This isn't what

I was asking for!" That was when I knew: those weren't my thoughts. They were His. He wasn't here to validate my complaints—He was here to challenge me to grow.

Ever since, I've continued journaling with God every morning. Over the years, His voice has only grown stronger, and I've become better at recognizing when it's Him speaking.

The morning of my backyard encounter, however, was different. It was the first time I spoke out loud to Him instead of through writing. And it wasn't just a conversation—it was much more powerful. I didn't just hear Him; I felt Him. I saw Him in a way I never had before. He was right there with me. And the voice I heard that day? It was the same voice I'd been hearing all those years.

It was Him.

My sheep listen to my voice.... John 10:27

The rest of that week, God made sure I knew He was working.

It started with food. For the past three months, eating had been a nightmare. I was stuck on a diet of vegetables because anything else—no matter how small—would cause my face and eyes to swell. Just days before, I'd finished recovering from yet another reaction. If I dared to eat anything beyond vegetables, it took four long days for my face to return to normal. I couldn't afford to look like that with important business meetings coming up. But God had told me I was healed.

At first, I didn't know what to do with that. Being healed felt like an impossibility. But then I talked to my son Michael.

"Mom, if God told you you're healed, then you are."

And that's what faith is, isn't it? Believing what we can't see. Trusting even when everything in your mind screams, "Don't do it! You'll regret it!" Faith doesn't always make sense, and in that moment, it didn't seem logical that I could suddenly eat without consequences. But I chose to believe anyway.

That Wednesday, I had plans with my mom and sister for our annual Mother's Day tradition: shopping and lunch. I had been concerned, wondering where we could go that had something I could safely eat. I had never realized how exhausting it was to live with food sensitivities.

The simple act of ordering from a menu had become a source of anxiety. Before my encounter with God, I would have stuck to my usual safe option: a plain plate of vegetables.

But now, things had changed. I was ready to trust that God had healed me. So, when we sat down at the restaurant, I didn't play it safe. I ordered a rice bowl—something I hadn't dared to eat in months, especially since rice had triggered a bad reaction the week before.

Lunch was delicious. Every bite felt like a victory. More than the food, I savored the feeling of being normal again. That little "what if" doubt crept up in the back of my mind, but I pushed it aside. *Nope*, I reminded myself, *God healed me.*

My mom and sister were amazed when I shared my story. They were thrilled to be sitting down to a meal with me again, while cautiously hoping I wouldn't have a reaction.

Later that afternoon, I had a board meeting at another restaurant. Before all this, I would have dreaded it. But now, I felt invincible. I believed. When fried calamari and Utica greens hit the table, I dug in, fully aware that fried food was a bold move. I was determined to prove to myself that God had performed a miracle.

And it worked. The next morning, my eyes and face were clear—no swelling, no redness, nothing. I couldn't stop smiling. The real test, though, was still to come: pizza and wings on Mother's Day. For months, my family had tiptoed around my food restrictions, ordering pizza only when I wasn't home, or I'd hide in the bedroom so I wouldn't smell it and be tempted. That day, though, I sat down with my family and indulged in pizza. And it was wonderful—pure, simple joy.

No reaction. I was healed. I had no doubt God had worked a miracle in me. I was in awe, humbled. How could I wrap my mind around the fact that the Creator of the universe had stepped into my life and given me this gift?

But God wasn't finished. He wanted to make sure I knew He was working. He sent two more signs that same week.

The first was about my business. In January, I'd lost a huge contract, and it devastated me. Yet, out of nowhere, I received an email saying I had a chance to win back that business. That's unheard of in my industry. Once a company moves on, that company doesn't look back for years. But this? This was God. I knew it. My son Michael was with me when I read the email, and I started jumping around like a kid. It wasn't just the business opportunity that filled me with joy—it was knowing that God was behind it. He was showing me that He was moving mountains in my life.

The second sign came in the form of a *New York Times* article titled, "Thousands Believe Covid Vaccines Harmed Them. Is Anyone Listening?" (May 2024). For four years, I had doubted the narrative we were being fed about the pandemic and the COVID shots. I had serious concerns and feared the truth was being covered up. I had been praying fervently for no one to be harmed and for God to expose what was going on. That article was published the same week, and I knew it was no coincidence.

In one week, God had tackled every major issue that had been tearing me apart: my health, my business, and my lingering doubts about the pandemic. He was checking them off one by one, showing me that He had been with me all along, orchestrating it all in His perfect timing.

With everything God did, you'd think I'd have no room for doubt. But you'd be wrong.

My rational, overthinking mind got in the way. When I tried to explain my experience to others—the healing, the vision, the messages—I couldn't find the words. It all sounded impossible. While I was in the middle of the encounter, there wasn't a shred of doubt. I *knew* it was God. But when I shared it with my family and close friends, the more I talked, the less real it sounded. Even to myself. I started hesitating to tell anyone, afraid they'd think I was making it all up.

The hardest part to explain was the vision. I'd find myself stumbling through my explanation, saying, "I saw something, but I didn't really *see* something." It wasn't a clear image; it was transparent, yet massive, larger than life. I'd try to describe it as a mountain-like shape, like an outline of Jesus. And I knew how crazy that sounded. But during the moment itself, there was no confusion. I knew it was God—not because of what my eyes saw, but because of what my heart felt. It was like my heart was about to burst. I had never felt that before. I was filled with awe, reverence, and peace, while also feeling completely unworthy.

Most of all, I knew it was Him because I recognized His voice.

Every time I tried to explain what happened to others, I felt a little silly and a lot frustrated. But in those moments of doubt, I'd remind myself of one thing: what God told me to do. "*Tell them anyway.*"

Someone asked me how I *knew* it was God, hinting that maybe it was something else. That question rattled me. What if it wasn't divine? What if it was something dark—something demonic? That's when my overthinking got the best of me, and doubt began to creep in.

I shared my concerns with Robin.

"Of course, you're doubting! That's the enemy attacking you," she said. "He doesn't want you to share this with others. He doesn't want you to believe this was God."

Despite her reassurance, the doubts kept growing, spiraling out of control. I started questioning everything. "What if my experience wasn't biblically sound? Doesn't the Bible say no one can see God? Maybe I shouldn't be sharing this at all."

Conflicted and overwhelmed, I decided I needed guidance from someone who knew the Bible much better than I did. I sent a message to my pastor, asking if he had time to meet.

That afternoon, I sat with Pastor Mike and his wife, Melissa, for over an hour. I read everything to them, word for word, exactly as I had written it down after the experience. I didn't want to embellish or misrepresent anything. I wanted them to hear the raw truth of what had happened—nothing more, nothing less.

When I finished, Pastor Mike looked genuinely amazed. He told me there was nothing in my account that made him believe my experience wasn't from God. He reassured me that a false encounter wouldn't bring the kind of peace and healing I had experienced. As we spoke, a sense of calm began to wash over me. I realized God had led me to seek his counsel.

Before we wrapped up our meeting, I expressed my hesitation about sharing the story with others. Pastor Mike gave me two pieces of advice that I'll never forget.

The first thing he touched on was Paul's warning in the Bible against boasting:

> *If I must boast, I will boast of the things that show my weakness.* 2 Corinthians 11:30

In other words, if there's anything worth boasting about, it's only because of God, not us. After I went home and reflected on that chapter, I realized God was reminding me that this entire experience wasn't about me—it was about Him. It would have been so easy to think, *God chose me, so I must be special.* But no, this was about bringing glory to Him, not elevating myself.

Then came Pastor Mike's second piece of advice, which hit home when I pressed him about sharing the vision. I wanted to know how to explain it, how to tell others about something so profound yet so hard to put into words. He cautioned me, saying, "Your story might freak people out. Years ago, someone gave me advice that's served me well: when speaking to the public—or even the press—never say anything you're not 100 percent sure of."

That advice was a game-changer. I realized I couldn't say with complete certainty what I saw that day. I couldn't describe it with absolute clarity. That realization brought me relief. It gave me permission to share my experience without the pressure of trying to explain exactly what I saw. I could still tell my story—just with a focus on the healing and what I *felt* rather than on what I *saw*.

Even my family agreed. Then, in the first draft of this book, I tried removing any mention of seeing or hearing God. I thought I could still tell the story without delving into the more mysterious aspects. But by doing that, I left out the most significant part: the vision, the greatest thing that's ever happened to me, the moment that changed me forever! My body had physically reacted to being in the presence of the Lord, and yet I was trying to omit that crucial part.

Why? Because it felt safer. I didn't want to put myself in a position to be mocked or ridiculed. But the truth is, the vision was everything, and without it, I wasn't telling the full story.

Leaving that out of my story never felt right. It was clear to me that God was working on my heart, nudging me, pushing me forward. I tried to hide from it, but He wouldn't let me. Over and over, I felt Him saying, "Tell them anyway." It became obvious that He had given me this gift not to keep to myself, but to share—no matter how uncomfortable that made me. I was trying to dim the light on the greatest experience of my life, on God's work. How could I think *that* was okay?

I prayed, "Forgive me, God, for feeling so weak. Please give me the strength to endure whatever may come when I share this."

If the world hates you, keep in mind that it hated me first. If you belonged to the world, it would love you as its own. As it is, you do not belong to the world, but I have chosen you out of the world. That is why the world hates you.
John 15:18–19

I already knew what it felt like to be hated in business, simply for being a woman. Maybe God had been preparing me all along when men treated me poorly, dismissing me as though I didn't belong.

If you are insulted because of the name of Christ, you are blessed, for the Spirit of glory and of God rests on you. 1 Peter 4:14

Looking back, I can't believe I considered hiding this incredible experience. God kept showing up in my life, proving His presence over and over. What became clear to me is that He's always with us—every moment of every day. I had been blind to that before. He doesn't want us to say a quick prayer and then go about our day as if He's not interested in being a part of it. He wants to be in *everything*. He wants us to open our hearts and tune into His presence constantly.

We are never truly alone—unless we choose to be. The enemy waits for us to leave God behind so he can attack our minds and hearts. I finally understand what it means to put on the armor of God. We're meant to carry His protection with us into every situation, trusting Him to guide us, defend us, and give us strength all day, every day.

Put on the full armor of God, so that you can take your stand against the devil's schemes. Ephesians 6:11

I didn't fully grasp that until this experience. I used to think God was too big and too powerful to be concerned with the small details of my life. I didn't want to "bother" Him. But He showed me that He *wants* to be involved in every aspect. We don't have to just grin and bear it, hoping things will eventually get easier someday. No, He wants to be with us and help us in the "here and now," to guide us, and to give us miracles in our daily lives. He wants to show us that everything good comes from Him, not from us. He wants the glory.

God is the master conductor of our lives. He weaves every thread together perfectly. Even when we don't realize it or acknowledge Him, He's still in control. We don't have to worry because He's got it all under His care until the day we return home to Him. The only time things get messy is when we try to take control away from Him.

I don't believe it was a coincidence that during this time, my Bible study group was going through the Book of Joshua. God performed miracles for Joshua and the Israelites, His chosen people, as long as they believed He was bigger than their problems. One of those miracles was the fall of Jericho. Jericho's walls were massive, seemingly impenetrable, giving the city every advantage. But God told His people that victory would be theirs if they just marched around the walls. That's all they had to do: march. And when they obeyed, the walls crumbled. God wanted to show them that He could make the impossible, possible.

That's the story God wants to share: He can do the impossible in our lives too, if we trust Him enough to let Him.

My health issue felt like my Jericho—a seemingly insurmountable obstacle that I had to believe God could heal me from miraculously. I conquered that battle only because I walked in faith, trusting that God wouldn't let me down. It's easy for people to say, "Have faith," but having genuine faith in times of trial is anything but simple. It's human nature to cling to what we can see and touch, fearing disappointment. But with God, anything is possible, especially when that "anything" aligns with His will. He does His best work when the odds are stacked against us.

The story of Joshua is also one of obedience, and God continued to pull and stretch my faith and willingness to obey. He prompted me to do something I didn't want to do: give my employees generous raises. At that time in 2024, we barely had any work, and I thought to myself, *This can't be God. He wouldn't want me to be financially irresponsible!* I hesitated, dragging my feet, wishing He would change His mind and give me a clear sign that it was okay not to follow through.

But then, I got my sign loud and clear. Our inspection machine broke down, and fixing it cost me more than the raises would have. Sure, it could have been a coincidence, but I felt this may have happened because I hadn't listened to His command.

So, I gave out the raises. I realized that I didn't want to mess with God's plans any longer.

Money was a bigger issue for me than I had realized. God also asked me to increase my giving to the church and set up automatic withdrawals. Although I had been giving, I liked having control over my donations, convincing myself that I wasn't fully committed to calling Redeemer Church my church yet. I thought, *If I have the power to stop or change my mind, I'm safer.* But now, looking back, I see how silly that was. I had control over the auto-debit mechanism. It was a "me" issue, my inner control freak rearing its ugly head.

God has a sense of humor too. After I increased my donation and set up the auto-withdrawal, I grabbed my purse on the way to church the next morning and found a $50 bill. I felt God nudge me, saying, "I want you to put that in the bucket today." I couldn't help but react, exclaiming in my kitchen, "You've got to be kidding me!"

I was frustrated, even angry, and I found myself in an adult temper tantrum. "Look at what I've already done. Isn't that good enough?" As I drove to church, I was unsure of my next move. When they passed around the buckets, I reluctantly reached for the $50, thinking, *Fine, You win.* But then, to my surprise, the bucket didn't come down my row! What are the chances? I thought, *Great! God's letting me keep the $50 after all.* But deep down, I knew He was testing my willingness to obey.

Eventually, I found someone at the end of the service and donated the $50. I felt a wave of peace wash over me, knowing God was pleased. It made me smile to think of His playful nature.

During one of my morning journaling sessions in the summer of 2024, God revealed to me why He was blessing me so abundantly: it was because of my past obedience. He reminded me of the New Age practices I had let go of months prior, when I felt Him urging me to stop. I had dabbled in things I was learning might open doors to spirits I didn't want to engage with. I wrestled with disbelief but ultimately decided it wasn't worth the risk. I had explored aligning chakras, energy healing, yoga, and meditation, believing they offered me what I needed without God's involvement. One of my employees even let me borrow crystals to put in my office, hoping they would bring prosperity. But one morning, I felt God tell me to remove them. It took me weeks to find the courage to tell my employee that I didn't want them anymore. I was more worried about offending her than about pleasing God. In the end, it was a nonissue; she took her crystals back without appearing to think anything of it.

God also reminded me that in January, I had surrendered my business to Him. When I lost the major contract and felt utterly crushed, my confidence shattered. I was devastated and hit an all-time low as a business owner, especially with our son Michael now working for us. I felt the pressure of everyone's livelihood being dependent on our success. I didn't know what to do except surrender my business completely to God. I told Him, "It's Yours. You'll have to show me what to do."

Every morning, I would pray, "God, please just get me through the day." I would pull out my journal and ask, "What do You want me to do today?" That's all I could manage—just one day at a time. I'd jot down the tasks He placed on my heart, then head to work to follow through.

My morning prayer time became my lifeline. He led, and I followed. He guided me to try new things in business, things I had never considered before. That's how the door opened to winning that business back.

Why would I ever think of reverting to *my* ways when *His* ways are so much better and smarter?

Chapter Seven
More Blessings

Over the next few weeks as May turned to June, God kept showing up in my life, not just with more blessings, but with corrections too. As I deepened my walk with Him, I began to see His corrections as blessings in disguise. One morning He showed me I was holding onto unforgiveness—especially toward my husband. At first, I didn't believe it, but as I reflected, I realized there were unresolved issues I'd never dealt with. Rob and I have been together since we were both 15 years old, so of course, there would be some baggage. But what surprised me was that I thought I had dealt with everything from our past. God was putting on my heart that I hadn't.

I dove into the Scriptures, searching for every verse on forgiveness. Time and again, the Bible reminded me that I wasn't perfect either, even though my pride had convinced me otherwise. I could always spot Rob's faults more easily than mine. But once I broke through that surface layer of denial and started seeing myself the way God does—flawed and in need of grace—everything became clearer.

If God could forgive me for my failings, how could I withhold that grace from Rob? I'm far from mastering this, but with God's help, I hope to become the wife God calls me to be.

I've always seen myself as a strong woman, someone who didn't need a man to complete her. I even used to say that if Rob ever treated me poorly, I'd simply divorce him. But deep down, I never wanted that. I've always wanted our marriage to work. I just had a skewed, worldly view of what marriage should be, something that could easily be swapped out if it wasn't meeting my expectations. Now, after more than 30 years together, there's no one I love, trust, or want by my side more than Rob.

No one ever explained marriage to me from a biblical perspective. I never realized what a precious gift God intended it to be. Reading Tim Keller's book *The Meaning of Marriage* was a turning point for me. It made me want to be a better wife and have a better marriage. The values in the book—what some might call old-fashioned—were timeless, pure, and beautiful. Keller spoke of sacrificial love and how far today's typical marriages fall short of that ideal.

He explained that God uses marriage as a tool to refine us, holding up a mirror to reveal our flaws and sins so that we can grow and transform. No one else can expose our shortcomings the way a spouse can. But the key is to do it with love, gentleness, and a heart intent on helping each other become who God created us to be.

I once heard someone say that your spouse becomes who you believe him or her to be. That means if I keep looking for the bad, then that's exactly what I'll keep getting more of. That hit home for me. I realized I had a part to play in feeling disappointed by Rob. It's easy to focus on the negative and complain, thinking Rob was the problem instead of me. But I've come to see that taking responsibility for *my* role in our marriage is what can turn things around. And with God's guidance, we're achieving that together.

***

I couldn't believe how often God showed up, in the most unexpected ways. I became laser focused on everything He was doing, and it was as though He was everywhere, guiding and blessing me at every turn. One person who shared my excitement was Robin. She became one of my closest confidants during this time. Every time something remarkable happened, she was as thrilled as I was.

One evening, I stopped by her house and mentioned how wild it was that, just a week before, my prayer request at Bible study had been to hear from God, and then He showed up in my backyard. Robin's eyes lit up as she grabbed her journal to check what she had written down that night. But what she found was different from what I remembered. Instead of my request to hear from God, she had noted that I asked for wisdom, guidance, and to be a good wife.

I paused, confused. *That didn't match what I had written in my journal.*

I didn't say much at the time, but it bothered me. For the rest of the evening, I felt unsettled. I had been so excited, feeling like God had answered my specific prayer to hear from Him. But now, it seemed that's not what I had actually asked for out loud. When I got home, I immediately checked my journal, and there it was, clear as day—my prayer had been to hear from God.

The next morning, I woke up around three a.m., as had become my routine during this season of my life. Early mornings had always been times of my clearest moments, when my mind felt sharp and alive. Looking back, I realize now that God was probably speaking to me in those quiet hours. I had been documenting my entire spiritual journey in those moments, determined not to miss a single detail.

That morning, I couldn't shake the difference between my version of the prayer request and what Robin had written down. I kept thinking, *Why didn't I say what I had written? Why did I change it?* I always make a point to write down my requests so I can mark when God answers my prayers.

Honestly, I was disappointed because it felt as though the story would have been better if our notes had matched perfectly. But then, in the middle of my frustration, God spoke to me. I heard Him clearly say in my spirit, "Don't you see? You don't need to say it out loud for Me to hear you."

Whoa! Once again, God blew me away. He took what had been bothering me and transformed it into something far more powerful. It wasn't about the notes matching; He wanted me to realize that I don't need to get every word right when I pray in front of others, as if my Bible study group were a prayer hotline and if I didn't say it out loud, God wouldn't respond. He wanted me to know that He always knows my heart. Exact words? They aren't necessary.

That truth has always been in the Bible, but I needed the reminder. From that moment, my prayer life transformed. I no longer worried about saying the perfect words, knowing God already understands my thoughts and concerns. All I have to do is open my heart and fully surrender to Him.

> *In the same way, the Spirit helps us in our weakness. We do not know what we ought to pray for, but the Spirit himself intercedes for us through wordless groans.* Romans 8:26

It always comes back to surrender—letting go of my ideas, my ways, my opinions. Letting go of the worries over my life, my marriage, my business. Surrendering it all. It's not always easy, but when I do surrender, life feels so much more peaceful. I never understood that before. No matter how much wisdom I think I have, God's is infinitely greater. Why would I ever stress and cling to control when I have Him? Yes, I still need to do my part, but I don't have to exhaust myself trying to fix every detail.

There's incredible peace in not needing all the answers. If my inner control freak had learned this sooner, maybe life wouldn't have been as hard as I made it.

***

Once I knew that God had healed me, I couldn't help but wonder *when* the miracle happened. Was it during my encounter with God in my backyard, or was it back at church on Sunday when I went up for prayer? So, I prayed and asked God to show me when it happened. God revealed to me that the healing took place on Sunday, and when He told me, "You are healed," on the Tuesday after, that was simply my confirmation. In that moment, my wonder vanished. His power is so majestic, yet we often stand in the way of receiving all He wants to give us.

It occurred to me how easily I could have missed the greatness of what God had done. I could have clung to the idea that I still had food issues and refused to step out in faith to eat the very things that were causing my reactions. Maybe without that faith, the miracle could have vanished. Or maybe I might have gone weeks without realizing I'd been healed, thinking it was due to a strict diet or that the problem had resolved itself. I could have completely missed the connection to my prayer at the altar and diluted the experience, not recognizing it for the miracle it was. It makes me wonder how many times that happens. How many miracles is God performing every day that go unnoticed? My gut tells me it happens all the time.

That week, I shared with Robin every detail of what God was doing in my life. She confessed that she was trying not to "covet" my experience, longing to hear from God as clearly as I was. We spoke almost daily, and in one of her texts, she said something that floored me: "God has been preparing you for this moment so you can tell your story." Her words took me by surprise because, just a couple of days earlier, God had told me the exact same thing. I hadn't shared that with anyone yet—not even Robin—because it scared me.

God had said to me, "This is what I've prepared you for." When I heard it, I was resistant, even scared, asking Him, "What do You mean? I don't understand. I need details." But He gave me no further explanation. So, when Robin said those exact words, I was stunned. I replied, "I can't believe you just said that. I haven't told anyone, but Saturday night when I couldn't sleep, I heard God say the same thing: 'This is what I've prepared you for.'" I admitted that I'd been freaking out a little over it. Then I added, "Apparently, you hear from God more than you realize." God had told Robin something she couldn't have known, confirming that He was answering her prayer to hear His voice.

The truth is, He speaks to all of us, all the time. That's why He gave us the Holy Spirit—to live inside us, to guide and communicate with us. But we have to open our hearts to Him and invite Him into our lives to truly experience that connection.

I believe this is the message God wants me to share with anyone who'll listen: He's speaking to us—all of us—every single day. But too often, we brush it off, thinking His whispers to us are our thoughts. When His voice doesn't match what we want to hear, we ignore it. And when it does, we assume it's our idea.

The truth is, many of us haven't learned how to tune in to God's voice, and that's because our minds are filled with so much noise. That's why reading the Bible is so important—it's like a direct line to God and the Holy Spirit within us. It clears our minds so we can focus on Him, not just on our situations. When we dig into the Bible and learn about God's character, about who He is and how He works, it becomes so much easier to recognize His voice when He speaks. He's in every moment, every detail, if we'd just slow down long enough to notice.

***

God showed up at supper club. I have a group of six close girl-friends, and we call ourselves the "supper club." We regularly meet for dinner, but God had never been part of the conversation—until now. Honestly, I was nervous to share what had happened to me. What would they think? What would they say?

I knew the questions were coming because they were aware of my food struggles. I hadn't been able to join them for a real meal in months. The last time, I had only a bowl of fruit while they enjoyed their dinners. So naturally, they'd want to know how I was suddenly able to eat out with them again.

I didn't go into detail, but I did tell them I had experienced a miraculous healing after asking for prayer at church. To my relief, they were incredibly supportive. No one made me feel like I was crazy, and we ended up talking about God for over an hour. It was probably one of the deepest conversations we've ever had. Normally, our dinners are filled with laughter that makes our stomachs ache, but this time, it was serious and heartfelt. Some of them opened up about their relationships with God, and it was beautiful to see that side of them. We connected on a deeper, more intimate level.

***

One of the greatest examples of God working things out for good is when my son was in a relationship that I wasn't sure about. I tried my best to connect with his girlfriend, but we struggled to form a bond. My son, who was usually full of joy, seemed to lose his light. He didn't seem happy, yet he was talking about marriage.

I feared the path he was on. I voiced my concerns, but he insisted. He was an adult, able to make his own choices—what could I do?

I could pray. I prayed and prayed for my son and his girlfriend. I asked God to change my heart if this was His plan. I had dreamed of having daughters-in-law to love, since I never had a daughter of my own, but this wasn't how I pictured it.

We're told to pray and cast our cares on God, but I struggled with that. I prayed, but I continued to worry. My son was pulling away, becoming someone whom I barely recognized. I feared I wasn't gaining a daughter but losing a son. I told God that if this was His plan, He would have to help me through it.

I was happy that this young lady had a close relationship with God—I had always prayed that my sons would marry women of faith. She loved the Lord and knew the Bible well, and I think that's what initially drew my son to her. It became my common ground with her. She even encouraged me to join a small group Bible study, something I never would've done on my own. I agreed, hoping it would bring us closer.

Honestly, I joined the group for all the wrong reasons, but that's the amazing thing about God—He used it for my good. Joining that Bible study turned out to be one of the greatest blessings in my life. Without her influence, I might never have taken that step. I thought I was fine with my relationship with God, but through studying His Word, my life started to change. God began transforming me, and He used her as the catalyst.

Eventually, I made peace with their relationship, and around the same time, my son told me he was ending it. God had a plan all along. He used this young woman to bring both my son and me closer to Him. For that, I'll always be grateful that she came into our lives.

***

Months earlier, when I first started attending Redeemer Church, I wasn't sure how I felt about it. The messages were solid, but I found the people a little over the top. I found it distracting when people yelled out during the service, agreeing loudly with the preacher. And some of the worshippers seemed, well, a bit out there. Once I saw a girl jumping up and down as though she was at a rock concert. That seemed excessive. Many people raised their hands, but there was this one petite woman I always seemed to notice in the front. She was tiny, but somehow, she managed to stretch her arms and hands high above everyone else during worship. I remember thinking, *You look so silly doing that.*

When I decided to join a Bible study, I texted one of the leaders, who kindly offered to drop off a spare study book at my office. Wouldn't you know it, the person who walked in to deliver the book was none other than "the crazy arm lady" from church. I couldn't believe it. *You've got to be kidding me*, I thought.

This was the day I met Robin.

There's no doubt in my mind that God set this up to show me just how wrong I'd been. I had thought all that outward worship was just for show, but meeting Robin changed everything. She had a genuine love for the Lord that was impossible to miss. She's one of the most sincere people I've ever known and has become one of my closest friends and a confidant throughout this journey.

Back then, my heart was still hardened, but I get it now. When God started moving in my life, I couldn't help but fall more in love with Him and feel a deep desire to worship. My heart shifted. Suddenly, worship music moved me to tears as I began to grasp the profundity of what Jesus did for us on the cross. He was tortured, abused, and abandoned, and He died so that we can spend eternity in paradise.

I started to feel His incredible love in a way I never had before. Once I let that love seep into my heart, the music became something I couldn't get enough of. It stirred me so deeply that raising my hands felt like the most natural thing in the world. I surrendered fully to everything God has to offer. I no longer wanted to live life on my terms but on His.

I even got baptized. As someone who'd been baptized Catholic, I was adamantly against getting baptized again. I said it was something I would *never* do. But God softened my heart. After my experience with Him, I wanted everything He had for me. I learned that the Greek word for "baptize" means "to immerse, submerge."[1] As an infant, I'd only been sprinkled with water. But baptism, I came to understand, is a believer's first outward sign of repentance and a way to identify with Christ's death, burial, and resurrection. Going under the water symbolizes the death and burial, and coming up represents the resurrection.

> *We were therefore buried with him through baptism into death in order that, just as Christ was raised from the dead through the glory of the Father, we too may live a new life.* Romans 6:4

The more I learned about God's view of baptism, the more I realized I had been missing out on a precious gift by not getting baptized by full immersion. It felt like an opportunity I didn't want to pass up. So, with my family and a small group of fellow believers there to support me, I took the plunge—literally. It was a beautiful experience, and I'm so glad I made that decision.

In just a few short weeks, I changed in ways I never expected. Now I understood what it means to be a "new creation" in Christ (2 Corinthians 5:17 ESV). I was different. I was new. God felt so close, almost tangible. He was everywhere, in everything I did. The truth is, He had been there all along—I just had been an obstacle in my path to Him, blocking myself from seeing Him.

It wasn't just about the miracle He worked in my life; the greatest gift of all has been the peace and joy that I'd been longing for my whole life. It's a peace that stays with me, even when things go wrong. And trust me, things *still* go wrong. Really, sometimes I feel as though I now have an even bigger target on my back. For years, the enemy had me exactly where he wanted me—taking my faith lightly, going through the motions. I'm not sure if he's attacking me more now, or if I'm just more aware when he's trying to mess with me. But, I remind myself, my God is so much bigger than anything Satan can throw at me. So, bring it on—I'm ready. Even in the hardest moments, something is

---

1 *Strong's Exhaustive Concordance, s.v. baptizó, #G907.*

different now. God is holding me, His peace is right there, and I can reach for it whenever I need to.

Looking back, I realize how foolish and stubborn I'd been for so many years. Life is so much sweeter with God in control. Why did I ever think I had to handle everything on my own? There's such a weight lifted knowing I don't have to do this by myself anymore. The most precious gift in the world is surrendering it all to Him, our holy Lord and Savior. I can't help but wonder, why didn't someone make me see what I was missing?

Chapter Eight
The Enemy

I've heard it said that we're either living for God or for Satan—there's no middle ground. The more I think about it, the more I realize how true that is. If the enemy had his way, he'd dominate and destroy our lives completely. Now that I'm more aware of this fact, I can't help but reflect on how this battle has played out over the years.

For the longest time, I didn't pay much attention to Satan or how he might be affecting me. I didn't think he was relevant—honestly, it even felt strange to say his name. But as I studied the Word of God, I started to understand just how sneaky, sly, and cunning he is. He's the master of deception, always working in the background, messing with our thoughts and emotions. The scary part is, he does the most damage when we're not even aware of his presence.

The Scriptures opened my eyes to how the enemy operates. It's like shining a light on his dirty tricks—once you see them, they're easier to spot. Looking back, I can now see all the ways I unknowingly gave him space in my life. Deception is his greatest weapon, and I was fully deceived. His influence was destructive, and I was blind to the turmoil and pain he was causing.

I still mess up all the time, and I know I'll continue to struggle with sin until the day Jesus takes me home. But I've grown so much with God. When I look back, I can see how far I've come. I was a wreck compared to where I am now, and I'm sharing my past ugliness in the hope that you might recognize ways the enemy could have a grip on your life.

People-Pleasing

I first realized Satan had a grip on me when I got honest about how much of a people-pleaser I was. I always tried to fit in, always wanted to be liked. The only place I could show my real, sometimes contradictory opinions was around family. Outside of that, I avoided conflict at all costs, never wanting to offend or disagree with others. But people-pleasing is a dangerous, slippery slope. It can easily lead us to compromise what we know deep down to be morally right.

Looking back, I can't help but wonder if I should have spoken up more during the pandemic. I didn't agree with the mandates or the masks or forcing people to do things against their will. I was heartbroken watching people lose their jobs for not complying. It felt like evil had a grip on the entire world, and yet, I stayed silent. I was too afraid to speak up.

That's the thing about people-pleasing—it can paralyze us in moments when our voices matter most. The enemy loves that because it keeps us from standing up for truth and what we believe in. It's something I'm still learning to overcome, but at least now I can recognize where I've been deceived and start breaking free from that grip.

Money and Success

For a long time, chasing money and success was my sole purpose in life. I put it above everything else, and while I achieved a certain level of success on paper, my life felt incredibly difficult—and often empty. There were countless days when I gave my family only the bare minimum. It was a constant internal struggle. I loved my family and yearned to spend time with them, but I kept convincing myself that there simply weren't enough hours in the day to get all my work done.

Now I realize that was one of Satan's lies, and I fell for it completely. I was stuck on the success hamster wheel that so many people find themselves on, spinning faster and faster while life passed me by. It's a hard truth to face, but acknowledging this deception has been a big step toward breaking free and rediscovering what truly matters.

Alcohol

For years, getting drunk and having a good time was my way of coping with a demanding week and the pressures of work. Honestly, I wasn't sure I even knew how to enjoy myself without alcohol. Being the designated driver on a night out felt like a punishment, and Rob and I were relieved when our son was old enough to pick us up after a night of drinking. Looking back, I regret exposing my kids to the sight of their parents overindulging.

The mornings after these nights were brutal. I'd wake up feeling like garbage, often dragging that feeling with me for days. I despised what I was doing to myself, yet I found myself repeating the same cycle week after week. I believed that a life without alcohol would be dull— yet another of the enemy's lies echoing in my mind.

Truthfully, alcohol created problems in my marriage. I hated it when Rob drank too much: it led to arguments. I can't help but think how much healthier and happier our marriage could have been without alcohol hanging over us. It was a barrier that clouded our connection and kept us from truly enjoying each other.

Do not get drunk on wine, which leads to debauchery. Instead, be filled with the Spirit. Ephesians 5:18

Lust/Flirting

I used to think flirting with men other than my husband was harmless as long as I didn't cross the line by sleeping with them. There were times when I got attention from other men, especially in the business world. For years, I found it a boost to the ego. But not all the attention was flattering—some men were downright creepy. Yet, I still allowed them to speak to me in ways I shouldn't have, convincing myself it was all in good fun.

Looking back, I realize how disrespectful that behavior was—not just to Rob, but to my marriage and to myself also. Instead of confronting the problems in my relationship when I felt disconnected, I let issues cause separation from my husband when we needed to grow closer.

God is clear: flirting isn't okay, and I see now how much I missed that truth in my pursuit of validation.

> *You have heard that it was said, "You shall not commit adultery." But I tell you that anyone who looks at a woman lustfully has already committed adultery with her in his heart.* Matthew 5:27–28

Entertainment

I saw violent and sexually explicit movies as harmless entertainment. However, I gradually began to see how these films hurt God's heart and realized I didn't want to consume them anymore. It became clear that filling my mind and heart with such content was not in line with what He desires for us.

Nowadays I'd rather curl up with a feel-good movie than subject myself to aggression, violence, and gore. Those kinds of films don't sit well with me anymore. I love to unwind with a great flick, but I've become more selective. I'm a sucker for a good romance, but God has reminded me to be cautious about any movie that tempts me to compare my relationship with a fictional one on screen. The enemy thrives on that kind of comparison, using it to sow dissatisfaction in our marriages—a dangerous trap.

The enemy also tries to convince us that sex is just fun between consenting adults, not the expression of the sacred intimacy God designed for husband and wife. At first, I found God's view of marriage a bit naïve, but as He transformed my heart, I began to appreciate the beauty and holiness of His perspective. Our bodies are precious to Him, and understanding that truth has shifted how I view relationships entirely.

Do you not know that your bodies are temples of the Holy Spirit, who is in you, whom you have received from God? You are not your own. 1 Corinthians 6:19

Anger

I believed it was perfectly fine to get angry when someone mistreated me. Standing up for myself in the face of what I saw as injustice felt justified. Honestly, I still struggle with this issue. You wouldn't want to be a fly on the wall when the airline loses my luggage or when Amazon messes up my order! In those moments, my less-than-graceful side tends to rear her ugly head. I often find myself lacking tolerance and the ability to extend grace.

Why? It's probably because I'm still grappling with pride and the belief that things should unfold *my* way. In those heated moments, I'm terrible at showing love to others, but I'm getting better at reaching out to God for help, asking Him to keep me calm and prevent me from becoming a hothead.

I'm learning that nothing is worth getting twisted up over. In the heat of the moment, it feels justified, but I've realized that I don't like looking back at those angry versions of myself. The same goes for times when I've argued with others, desperately trying to prove I'm right. It's just another trap! I can only imagine how much the enemy relishes seeing me get worked up and act like a lunatic.

Showing anger and unloving behavior is not who God calls us to be. I know I have a long way to go, but recognizing that my true battle is against the enemy helps me keep myself in check a little longer.

For our struggle is not against flesh and blood, but against the rulers, against the authorities, against the powers of this dark world and against the spiritual forces of evil in the heavenly realms. Ephesians 6:12

Jesus compared anger to murder. He taught that the same evil spirit that causes someone to feel hatred also causes someone to murder.

You have heard that it was said to the people long ago, "You shall not murder, and anyone who murders will be subject to judgment." But I tell you that anyone who is angry with a brother or sister will be subject to judgment. Again, anyone who says to a brother or sister, "Raca," is answerable to the court. And anyone who says, "You fool!" will be in danger of the fire of hell. Matthew 5:21–22

Lord God, help me to respond more the way Jesus would!

Envy

As I mentioned previously, I never saw anything wrong with wanting what others had. I saw it as a great motivator. But now I see that envy is a trap that keeps us unsatisfied and unhappy. I was suffering from a severe case of "comparison-itis." No matter what I had or achieved, I could always find someone who had more, or better versions of it. It was a clever game of Satan's, feeding my desire with an endless cycle of "I want, I want, I want." Yet, none of what I desired ever filled the void inside me.

Only God Himself could do that. Through my journey, I've gained a valuable perspective. God let me achieve success, and I learned that reaching the finish line wasn't all it was cracked up to be. As long as I focused on accumulating things and chasing success, I lost sight of God. That's always the enemy's aim—to divert our gaze away from the Lord.

Profanity

I used to believe there was nothing wrong with swearing. I thought a well-placed f-bomb added emphasis to a conversation. I knew my swearing was unladylike because every so often I'd try to clean up my language, but those attempts never lasted more than a day. Before I knew it, I'd slip right back into my old foul-mouthed habits.

However, when God transformed my heart, my language also began to change. I'd love to say I never slip up, but that wouldn't be true. Still, my speech today is far from what it was. The best part? I didn't have to do anything special. The change happened effortlessly, which makes it clear to me that God was working within me.

Let there be no filthiness nor foolish talk nor crude joking, which are out of place, but instead let there be thanksgiving. Ephesians 5:4 ESV

Pride

For a long time, I thought my achievements were solely the result of hard work. I believed in God and acknowledged that He controlled the big stuff, but I rationalized that our having free will meant we were in charge of most things. It's not like anyone ever taught me that God governs everything; I had to learn it through the Bible.

As I delved into the Scriptures, God's master craftsmanship became unmistakably clear. That's why I can't get enough of the Bible—God never fails to amaze me. There's nothing like witnessing His handiwork and watching His plan unfold in real time. The Bible opened my eyes to the truth: nothing we do surprises God, and believers can't derail His master plan for our lives. Of course, when we stray from His path, we might find ourselves dealing with extra bumps and bruises along the way, but in the end, we aren't as powerful as we pretend. God is always in control.

I now understand that my talents and accomplishments are all gifts from Him. What I once saw as my cleverness and resourcefulness were His works through me. I used to pride myself on having healed my rosacea through my training as a certified detox specialist, thinking it was all my doing. I put in the effort of eating differently. I loved telling people I'd healed myself, but now I question that. *Was* it me, or was God guiding my journey all along?

Confronting the reality that my worldly views didn't align with biblical truth felt like a wrecking ball smashing through my life. It was uncomfortable. Every turn brought a new revelation, smacking me in the face. The Bible warns us that we all tend to want to be the god of our lives, and no one is immune to the temptation of choosing his or her way over God's.

In his pride the wicked man does not seek him; in all his thoughts there is no room for God. Psalm 10:4

The Lord detests all the proud of heart. Be sure of this: They will not go unpunished. Proverbs 16:5

We all, like sheep, have gone astray, each of us has turned to our own way; and the Lord has laid on him the iniquity of us all. Isaiah 53:6

If anyone thinks they are something when they are not, they deceive themselves. Galatians 6:3

For by the grace given me I say to every one of you: Do not think of yourself more highly than you ought, but rather think of yourself with sober judgment, in accordance with the faith God has distributed to each of you. Romans 12:3

My biggest battle is with my pride, which often manifests as my desire to be right. Knowing that helps me keep in mind whom I'm fighting against. In the heat of the moment, I have to ask myself: "Is this argument worth turning my husband into a punching bag just to prove I'm right?" *Spoiler alert*: It never is. Even if I "win," I lose if it leaves him feeling badly about himself and our relationship.

Pride is a tough nut to crack. I'm realizing that whenever I have a problem with someone or something, pride is lurking beneath the surface. It's a constant reminder that victory isn't about being right; it's about nurturing our connection and lifting each other up.

Where there is strife, there is pride, but wisdom is found in those who take advice. Proverbs 13:10

New Age Practices

I was ensnared by a variety of New Age practices—things like reiki, yoga, crystals, energy medicine, horoscopes, mediums, and fortune-telling. Although I recognized these as spiritual practices, I never paused to consider the "spirits" I might be inviting into my life. I didn't worship false gods like Buddha, so I thought I was in the clear. I believed that my faith in God provided me with a protective shield.

But the Bible is clear: God doesn't want us to heal ourselves or use anything else to bring on good fortune. Jesus is the true healer and provider.

> *The Spirit clearly says that in later times some will abandon the faith and follow deceiving spirits and things taught by demons.* 1 Timothy 4:1

> *See to it that no one takes you captive through hollow and deceptive philosophy, which depends on human tradition and the elemental spiritual forces of this world rather than on Christ.* Colossians 2:8

> *Come to me, all you who are weary and burdened, and I will give you rest.* Matthew 11:28

I was surprised to discover how often the Bible gives examples of people engaging in what they think are "innocent" activities, only to find out that God sees them as worshipping false gods. These instances, detailed in the Old Testament, ultimately led to God's wrath.

> *But they rebelled against me and would not listen to me; they did not get rid of the vile images they had set their eyes on, nor did they forsake the idols of Egypt. So I said I would pour out my wrath on them and spend my anger against them in Egypt.* Ezekiel 20:8

> *Be careful to do everything I have said to you. Do not invoke the names of other gods; do not let them be heard on your lips.* Exodus 23:13

I used to think that the Old Testament was irrelevant and outdated, but the more I read it, the more I realized how deeply relevant it is to our lives today. God knew exactly what He was doing when He inspired those words. There's not a single passage in the Bible that doesn't hold significance for us.

Sometimes, we might not recognize what God deems as idol worship or what activities could inadvertently open doors to demonic influence, even when that's the last thing we intend. I couldn't see any wrongness in my actions, but those were the very cracks in my foundation that the serpent looks for to gain a foothold in our lives. The Bible warns us that ignorance is no excuse.

> *My people are destroyed from lack of knowledge. Because you have rejected knowledge, I also reject you....* Hosea 4:6

God extends His grace, but once you learn the truth, you can't unlearn it. You can choose to turn away from God's ways and risk the consequences, or you can recognize that this newfound knowledge is God's way of inviting you to be closer to Him and away from harm. Remember, God is ultimately in the business of redeeming and restoring His people. Pain can be an opportunity.

If something has popped into your mind or triggered you as you read these words, it might be God speaking to you. Be open to that. God often places small obstacles in our path before presenting us with bigger challenges—perhaps He's already trying to get your attention.

Here's the beauty of our Lord: All you have to do is reach out in prayer and be honest. You might say, "God, I'm struggling with what I'm feeling right now. Is this You trying to get my attention? I'm not sure what steps to take next. Please guide me and help me remove what needs to be removed from my life."

God's Wrath

The Bible warns us of God's wrath, revealing how destructive He can be when we continue to defy His ways. This wasn't a topic I liked to dwell on; it was easier to believe that God's anger wasn't something to fear. I preferred to see Him as only a loving Father, eager to grant my every heart's desire. But now I see that mindset was what kept me bound.

I had been treating God more like a genie in a bottle, kept on stand-by until I needed something. But as I spent more time in the Word, I saw that this isn't at all who God is. He has limits, and when we stray too far from His path, He can and will bring judgment. History shows us entire generations wiped out by His hand.

One night, a fierce thunderstorm jolted me awake. The power went out, and the house shook with each crash of thunder. I felt a fear deep in my core, and for some reason, my mind went straight to the idea of God's wrath. It was just a storm, but it felt like the sky itself was angry. The sheer force of it was overwhelming, and I couldn't help but imagine how much more powerful and terrifying God's anger must be.

I can't shake the thought of how angry God might be with the world right now. It's in chaos. With the constant promotion of abortion and transgenderism, I doubt He's pleased. The Scriptures warn us that wisdom begins with the fear of the Lord, yet most of the world refuses to heed that warning.

The fear of the Lord is the beginning of knowledge, but fools despise wisdom and instruction. Proverbs 1:7

I wish I could say that once I saw all the ways the enemy was attacking me, I never acted out of line again. But that's far from the truth. I'd love to tell you that after my encounter with God, I became a flawless reflection of Jesus, and my life turned into rainbows and sunshine. Not even close.

My business kept spiraling downward, and a deep rift in my family left me heartbroken. I still get frustrated and moody. I still overreact. Some days, it feels like life is hitting me from all sides. And I've realized that the enemy's target is still on my back—maybe even more so now. He hates when our relationship with God deepens.

The difference now is that I've accepted that I'm naturally inclined to sin and want to do things my way instead of God's. I no longer believe that I can reach perfection in this life. I've come to terms with the fact that I'm a mess—and will be until the day I go home to the Lord. And with that acceptance came an overwhelming sense of peace and freedom. That is what truly broke the chains. That is what surrendering to the Lord looks like.

If we confess our sins, he is faithful and just and will forgive us our sins and purify us from all unrighteousness. 1 John

Chapter 7 of the Book of Joshua reminds us that after a great victory, we're often vulnerable to a great fall or backsliding. It's when we become bigger targets for the enemy. My miraculous healing may have put me in that position, and the Lord teaches us to be vigilant in times like that. The enemy's attacks don't come only from the outside—they also come from within, from the evil that resides in our hearts.

We often look for answers outside ourselves, but the real challenge is within. Until we face the truth that we are part of the problem—that the seeds of evil lie within our hearts—we'll never grasp why life on this side of eternity is so difficult. God gave us a perfect world, but our sinful nature shattered it. Like Adam and Eve, who had everything but chose to reach for the one forbidden thing, we will always want more. This rebellion is something we'll struggle with until the day we return to the Lord. Only then, in His presence, will we be restored to the perfection God intended. By placing our faith in Jesus, believing that He bore the weight of our sins, we are promised a return to paradise.

We're rebellious by nature—it's a sickness that won't be cured until Jesus returns. I've always been a rebel; when someone told me I couldn't do something, I made it my mission to prove that person wrong. I used to think that was one of my best qualities, but now I see that's not always the case.

But here's the good news of Joshua chapter 7: in the middle of our greatest crashes, we often find our greatest blessings. In our darkest moments, we develop true intimacy with God. No matter the battle I face, it's so much easier to endure when God is by my side. He truly does work everything for our good if we trust Him. Now, when I'm facing a challenge, I have more peace. Instead of panicking, I wonder what God is up to, knowing He's in control. Joshua fought his battles on his knees, facedown before the Lord, and that's how I try to face mine now too.

When life gets tough and everything feels overwhelming, all I want is to spend time with God. His presence brings me peace and soothes the pain in my heart. I pour out my feelings, telling Him, "I'm scared.

I don't know what to do. Please help me. Guide me. Help me be kind when I feel terrible. Help me get out of my own way. Help me get out of Your way."

Sometimes, God responds with peace. At other times, He brings correction. Sometimes, He's gentle; at other times, His words are blunt. One day, I was stressing over a work task my son was handling, one I thought I should be doing instead. I had more experience and felt I could handle it better, that it would cost us less if I took over the negotiations. But I heard God say, "Stop—you're operating from a mindset of scarcity, not abundance."

I try to listen and obey whenever God corrects me. The Bible warns that disobedience is sin, and when we sin, we distance ourselves from God. That's where I never want to be.

> *But your iniquities have separated you from your God;*
> *your sins have hidden his face from you, so that he will*
> *not hear.* Isaiah 59:2

I don't want to give God any reason to turn away from me. I know He still loves us when we mess up, but He'll also let us learn the hard way if that's what it takes. I don't want to live that way anymore. I don't want sin creeping into my life or my business. Sin is what destroys everything, and I so deeply want my life and work to run smoothly under God's guidance.

Through this journey, I tried to figure out what God was up to, rationalizing everything to make sense of it. But then I realized that God doesn't fit into one of the boxes I use to understand life. He's beyond that. I had to stop letting my mind get in the way and just bask in His glory, feeling the joy of His incredible gifts. He moved so powerfully in my life—He healed me, changed me, gave me peace, and showed me how intricately He's weaving every detail of my story. His plan is already written; I need only walk it out in faith.

We can't always see what God is doing by looking forward, and we shouldn't try. Instead, we need to walk forward with trust and faith. It's only when we look back that we can see what an amazing Master He is. I've been transformed—my heart, thoughts, and desires are completely different now. I want what God wants, not what I used to think was best. I don't want to be in charge anymore. I don't want to be the master of my life. I've surrendered my life to God and His will.

I used to be a control freak, always overachieving and never satisfied. But now, I've found the peace and contentment that only God can give. He's all any of us needs to survive the chaos of life. When God told me that this journey was part of what He had prepared me for, I started to wonder if that's why I had been writing everything down. What started as personal journal notes kept growing into more and more. One day, I turned to Rob and said, "I think I'm supposed to write a book."

God gave me this unbelievable gift, but it's not something I'm meant to keep to myself. I've already expressed my worries to Him—how people might think I'm crazy for sharing my experience. But God clearly told me to *tell them anyway*. I'm nervous about what's ahead, especially with exposing so much of myself. But I know surrendering to God is how I want to live my life. The gift I received is something God wants everyone to know is available to him or her too.

As I continue this walk, God is refining me. I'm becoming less concerned with how others see me, less afraid of being labeled a "Jesus freak" or a "Bible thumper." I'm becoming okay with that (slowly). This is too big to lock away in my heart. The Bible warns us that those who love God will face persecution, but I'm learning that's a small price to pay for the incredible joy of knowing Him and living in His will.

In fact, everyone who wants to live a godly life in Christ Jesus will be persecuted. 2 Timothy 3:12

This book was written entirely under God's power and guidance. I tried to write years ago—I always felt there was a book inside me—but never got far. I'd start, get a couple chapters done, and then it would fall apart. Writing was a struggle. But this time, it was different. The words flowed out of me. It's all God, and He deserves every bit of the credit.

Incredibly, I finished the first draft a month after my encounter with Him. I truly believe it was God waking me up at three a.m. on so many mornings, saying, "It's time to write." There's no way I could have done this on my own. Even now, as I type these words, I can't help but wonder what God is up to.

Chapter Nine
COVID-19

W hat I'm about to share in this chapter is hard for me to discuss. It's something I've never spoken about publicly before. I hid my views so as not to offend or put a target on my back. During the COVID-19 pandemic, I decided not to get the vaccine, despite the intense pressure to do so. It was one of the hardest decisions I've ever made; it nearly broke me. But that struggle also drove me to reach for my Bible as a place of refuge and guidance.

Only another non-vaxxed person can understand the ridicule and isolation that came with that decision. I no longer felt that I fit in with the world I had known my whole life. Every news outlet, every conversation, seemed to paint people like me as outcasts. We were demonized and ridiculed. Suddenly, I found myself deemed unworthy of participating in society.

Living in New York made it worse. I couldn't enter certain buildings and restaurants or attend events. I wasn't allowed to participate in local business meetings, and after completing an eight-month business program in New York City, I wasn't able to attend the graduation or the celebrations.

So why did I make that decision? It wasn't just about being cautious about what I put in my body. The truth is, I never felt at peace about it. The vaccine was developed too quickly, and no matter how much I prayed, I felt a strong conviction not to get it.

One afternoon in June of 2021, I thought I was having a heart attack, which only turned out to be anxiety. The experience at the ER was traumatizing. The doctor grilled me about my vaccination status, as if only that mattered. I tried to explain my reasoning, but that didn't stop him from trying to shame me every time he walked back into the room. That day something shifted in me. I started to feel deeply uncomfortable with the world around me.

Media comments cut deep. One morning after my son left for school, I collapsed on the floor, sobbing. The pressure and hatred were unbearable. I begged God to make it stop.

It wasn't just affecting me—it was impacting my children, my parents, and other family members who also chose not to get the vaccine. Watching them experience the same hurt and rejection made it harder. We were ridiculed by the media, which showed people saying that the unvaccinated didn't deserve medical treatment if they got sick. It was terrifying.

I lived in constant fear. I worried about my family getting into an accident or needing emergency care. I learned everything I could about natural medicine, preparing for the worst. My parents were in their 70s, and the fear of being unable to protect them consumed me.

Some vaxxed family members were angry with those who weren't. Friends cut ties. I couldn't believe what was happening. I even considered closing my business and moving away from New York altogether. I started thinking about buying land in the middle of nowhere, just to escape the madness.

People kept saying, "Just get the shot. What's the big deal?" But for me, it *was* a big deal. I believed something much deeper was happening. The government wasn't just *encouraging* the vaccine; it was *forcing* it, and I couldn't shake the feeling that something was wrong.

Owning a business was a blessing. Rob and I didn't have anyone forcing us to comply with mandates. But our friends did. They were pressured to comply to keep their jobs, and I watched as their freedom was slowly stripped away. The more it was forced, the less I trusted it.

My youngest son, Matthew, was in high school, and he also experienced the pressure. At first, the messages were mild, but they intensified. I worried about whether he'd be kicked out of school or prevented from graduating. Protecting him from feeling like an outcast was one of the hardest things I faced as a mom.

Watching him and his friends play sports outside in the heat with masks on felt like a cruel joke.

Yet, amidst the chaos, there was a bright side. I connected with other parents who felt the way Rob and I did. Those friendships were a lifeline, and they kept me sane. COVID-19 became my wake-up call; something bigger was at play. If this product was so good, why did the government need to force it?

The more I learned, the more I questioned. The bribes, the mandates, the push from the media—it all felt "off." Pharmaceutical companies were making billions—with full liability protection. They can't be sued if they screw up, so where's the incentive to make a product safe? I began to see a bigger, more sinister picture, one that shook my trust in the systems I'd always believed in.

Before COVID-19, I rarely questioned a doctor's recommendation or a vaccine. But after everything I had witnessed, I could no longer ignore the uneasy feeling in my heart. It was time to say no to this one, no matter how hard the world pushed back.

What I had learned from ALS patients years prior made me uncomfortable. More than one patient told me about terrible health issues that began after getting certain vaccines. It forced me to confront something I didn't want to see. I never wanted to believe that I should question the vaccines my children were getting. For the first time in my life, I wondered if some of their ingredients might be harmful. I also began to question why my generation had received far fewer vaccines, yet we were still thriving. Our children seem to be dealing with many more chronic issues and allergies than we did as kids.

These questions arose years before the pandemic, but they played a significant role in my decision not to get the COVID vaccine. Not to mention, I spent an entire year in misery, eating nothing but fruits and vegetables to detox from past medications and years of poor eating habits. The thought of putting something into my body that could undo all that hard work didn't sit right with me.

There were moments when I was upset with God for putting me on this path. I didn't want to know what I was learning, didn't want to feel doubt about or mistrust our medical system. Life had been easier when I didn't question anything and just followed orders, so to speak, doing what was expected of me. Questioning things and going against the grain felt like an overwhelming burden I wasn't sure I was strong enough to carry.

Yet, the Scriptures teach that we grow through our struggles, developing a character like Jesus, who also endured great suffering during His time on earth.

> *He was despised and rejected by mankind, a man of suffering, and familiar with pain. Like one from whom people hide their faces he was despised, and we held him in low esteem.* Isaiah 53:3

The pandemic opened my eyes to a battle I had never fully seen before—a battle that felt evil. For the first time in my life, I witnessed governmental manipulation, censorship, and corruption, and it shook me to my core. It felt as though the world was unraveling, and I was scared. But in that fear, I clung to my Bible as never before. As difficult as that time was, I wouldn't change it because it brought me to where I am today. It deepened my relationship with God. Through diving into His Word, Christ became the center of my life—my strength, my protector, and my peace.

My greatest fear came from believing that evil was winning. But as I read the Bible, I found reassurance that God knew exactly what was happening. It was already written about. He was aware of the suffering, the tears, and the oppression we were facing. Seeing my fears reflected in the Scriptures gave me peace. God was saying, "I know; I understand." That understanding gave me the strength to face it all.

Again I looked and saw all the oppression that was taking place under the sun: I saw the tears of the oppressed— and they have no comforter; power was on the side of their oppressors—and they have no comforter. And I declared that the dead, who had already died, are happier than the living, who are still alive. But better than both is the one who has never been born, who has not seen the evil that is done under the sun. Ecclesiastes 4:1–3

God has always known the struggles His people would face— nothing catches Him off guard. He understands exactly what we are up against.

What has been will be again, what has been done will be done again; there is nothing new under the sun. Ecclesiastes 1:9

When hardships come, it doesn't mean evil is winning. Instead, it means God has allowed it for a greater purpose, often to bring us closer to Him. He is the master of every detail, and even in our darkest moments, His plan is unfolding.

The Bible reminds us that the enemy roams the earth, seeking to devour and destroy, but God remains in control, guiding us through every trial with purpose.

Be alert and of sober mind. Your enemy the devil prowls around like a roaring lion looking for someone to devour. 1 Peter 5:8

If we reach for the things of this world rather than the things of God, then bad things can happen. Bad things will happen anyway. The greatest secret to handling them is becoming obedient soldiers who seek God and His ways every day.

If you are willing and obedient, you will eat the good things of the land. Isaiah 1:19

Now all has been heard; here is the conclusion of the matter: Fear God and keep his commandments, for this is the duty of all mankind. Ecclesiastes 12:13

Every day, we need to fill ourselves with the Word of God by opening the Bible. There's no substitute for it. Podcasts and devotionals are great tools that can help us dig deeper, but opening the Bible is our direct line to God. Yes, it may be more challenging to understand scripture over a devotional, but the effort is worth it—what we gain from it will far exceed the work put in.

I know this because reading the Bible changed my heart and made me fall more in love with God. It was through His Word that I truly got to know Him and began to hear His voice. That love stirred a deeper obedience in me, a desire to remove anything from my life that wasn't aligned with Him. This is what unlocked everything for me, including my miraculous healing and the indescribable joy and peace I now experience.

God didn't speak to me or heal me because I'm special. He made that clear. He offers the same to everyone willing to open his or her heart to Him. It took me over five decades to receive this gift, but God was always there, patiently waiting for me to surrender and accept Him fully. I had been blocking Him, caught up in the ways of the world, thinking I had a solid relationship with God—but I had no idea what I was missing. He wanted to show me so much more and wants to do the same for all of us. That's the message He gave me: to tell people about the gifts that are waiting for them.

Chapter Ten
Next Steps

A real, beautifully intimate faith relationship with God is possible. But how do we dive deeper into faith? How do we learn to feel God's presence more intimately, especially when we don't even know what we're missing? The first step is to accept Him and give up the idea that we have all the answers. We must believe that Jesus Christ was a real Man who walked this earth, and the evidence is unmistakable for those willing to see it. He endured the most agonizing death in human history, taking on the punishment that each of us deserves. Yes, we deserve it. The truth is, we're not as good as we often like to believe. Recognizing our flaws and sinful nature is where the door to understanding begins to open.

We must also grasp the truth that He rose from the dead, emerging from the grave to reveal Himself to over 500 witnesses. Hallelujah! In doing so, God demonstrated the most unimaginable act of love. He became flesh and paid the ultimate price so that we could step into Heaven and live eternally in paradise with Him.

This concept is perhaps the hardest to comprehend: we don't have to die. When I began to understand this, my mind was blown. Believers in Jesus Christ don't experience death in the same way as others; instead, we pass through to Heaven and ultimately spend eternity with God in what the Bible describes as paradise and the new earth.

The Bible tells us that Jesus conquered death. Although I had heard this phrase many times, it never sank in—probably because I hadn't studied the Bible deeply. This can't be spoon-fed. It's through the Holy Spirit and engaging with the Word of God that we start to grasp this profound truth. When I finally "got" it, I was astonished: we don't have to die if we choose to live for God! Death is the one thing we assume is inevitable, the one thing that terrifies most people. But once that light bulb goes off and we begin living with this new knowledge, everything shifts.

The Bible paints a picture of returning to Eden, restoring the world to its original state before the fall of man. The new earth will have no curse of sin—no sickness, suffering, death, or evil. Sign me up! Before I immersed myself in the Scriptures, the idea of "Heaven" felt like a fairy tale. But now, I understand it, and I'm excited about what is to come. It far surpasses this fallen world.

> *See, I will create new heavens and a new earth. The former things will not be remembered, nor will they come to mind.* Isaiah 65:17

> *Never again will there be in it an infant who lives but a few days, or an old man who does not live out his years; the one who dies at a hundred will be thought a mere child; the one who fails to reach a hundred will be considered accursed. They will build houses and dwell in them; they will plant vineyards and eat their fruit.* Isaiah 65:20–21

> *"He will wipe every tear from their eyes. There will be no more death" or mourning or crying or pain, for the old order of things has passed away.* Revelation 21:4

*Then the angel showed me the river of the water of life,
as clear as crystal, flowing from the throne of God and of
the Lamb down the middle of the great street of the city.
On each side of the river stood the tree of life, bearing
twelve crops of fruit, yielding its fruit every month. And
the leaves of the tree are for the healing of the nations.*
Revelation 22:1–2

This doesn't mean our hearts don't break when we lose someone we love. The hardest part of life is enduring the absence of those we cherish. Yet, the hope of being reunited with them can bring comfort amid the pain. Scriptures suggest that believers will recognize one another in eternity. Take, for instance, the moment when Jesus, after His resurrection, called out to Mary in John 20:16: "Jesus said to her, 'Mary.' She turned toward him and cried out in Aramaic, 'Rabboni!' (which means 'Teacher')." She recognized Him.

If we focus on this truth daily, a new world will open up before us. Paradise with the Lord is where I'm headed, and the obstacles I face along the way no longer hold power over me. My final destination is going to be incredible.

I liken it to planning a trip or that dream vacation. Life goes on— we work, run errands, tackle problems—but there are moments when our thoughts drift to that upcoming adventure. We can't help but anticipate what it will be like when we finally get there. Living with an eye on spending eternity with God is like that; each day brings something to look forward to and rejoice in.

Without exploring the Bible, you can't fully grasp this truth. You might understand it intellectually, but without the Holy Spirit and the commitment to read God's Word, you won't know it in your heart. I was once in that place, unaware of how much I didn't know—until one day, I did. Maybe you're in the same situation, even if you're a believer. There are deeper levels of connection with God that He longs to reveal to each of us.

I wish I had made this shift long ago, but everything I endured was part of God's grand design. All my roads led me to here; the failures and heartbreaks are woven into my story. I needed to experience pain to reach out for Him. It took me believing I knew everything to realize how little I did understand. He was ready to reveal Himself back then, but I wasn't open to it.

He is ready, willing, and able to show Himself to you too. He wants you to hear His voice and be led by Him. You just need to clear away the barriers that block Him and get out of your own way.

Chapter Eleven
Not Quite the End

I thought I had wrapped up this book. I believed I was finished. Yet, the very week I completed the last page, an unsettling feeling crept in. Everything started to bother me. Work felt overwhelming, and things at home became sources of frustration. My dog was sick, I had looming deadlines and projects due, and I could feel myself slipping behind. I had just completed a book about finding peace from the Lord, but I felt anything but peaceful.

What was happening?

Was the enemy attacking me now that I had finished the book? My pride kicked in, insisting, "It must be good if the enemy is trying to stop it."

But it wasn't the enemy. It was God nudging me back into alignment. After finishing the book, I was riding high, convinced I had discovered something profound and eager to share it. So why was I feeling so "off"? Something felt amiss, but I couldn't put my finger on it. I reached out to Robin, hoping to chat with her, perhaps to unravel what was going on.

I once again see why God emphasizes the importance of surrounding ourselves with a godly community. After talking it out with Robin, the answer became clear. Through her, God revealed that the moment I thought I had it all figured out was the moment I completely missed the point.

In my excitement of feeling "done," I had inadvertently detached myself from the vine.

> *I am the vine; you are the branches. If you remain in me and I in you, you will bear much fruit; apart from me you can do nothing.* John 15:5

I found myself doing exactly what I had cautioned against. I became confident in what "I" had just accomplished. I had written a book, and I thought, *I've got this, God; I'll take it from here.* I didn't even realize I was slipping back into that mindset.

God asks us to depend on Him completely, yet my instinct is to figure things out on my own, to do things *my* way. I'm beginning to understand how challenging it is to stay connected to the vine. It requires me to "re-surrender" every single day. My flesh rebels at the thought of relying on *anything*—or *anyone*—including God. Honestly, I struggle with how to embrace that dependency.

It takes a daily mental reset. I need the Lord to dismantle the self-confidence and self-reliance I've worked so hard to achieve over the course of my life. It's about laying everything before Him each day and mustering the courage to acknowledge my flaws and the dark desires within me. I often yearn to be done with God's lessons for me. My life has always felt as though it was one interminably long to-do list, with the goal of getting things checked off and done so that I can finally earn my moment of relaxation.

But God has shown me I'll never truly be "done" until I'm with Him.

You know those sayings that encourage us to enjoy the journey, like "Getting there is half the fun"? Well, that's not me. I don't relish airplane rides on the way to anywhere; I just want to get off that plane and back on solid ground. I'm discovering how poorly I handle being a work-in-progress. Perhaps that's the point—God wants me to understand that without Him, I *can't* enjoy the journey. I may never be the easygoing type, but my primary job is to stay connected to Him, and I can only do that by seeking His help daily. So, I pray. I must pray every morning:

Lord God, help me. Without You, I will mess up this day. I will think I know better. Please keep me humble and attached to You. Help me to hear Your voice and never walk against Your will for my life.

I know my life is so much better with You in control instead of me. Help me to stop fighting it. Break my rebellious spirit of control and my resistance to full dependency on You.

Thank You for loving me enough to save me from myself. Help me to surrender this day to You.

In Jesus' holy and precious name, I pray.

Amen.

I hope that sharing my journey blesses and inspires you! My prayer is that you not only study the Bible, but also fall in love with it so much that you can't get enough of it. May God open your heart to all the incredible things He has in store for you.

Are you ready? Don't waste another moment—jump on God's exhilarating roller coaster of life! I'm beyond excited for you. His plan for your life will be unlike anything you've ever envisioned—infinitely better than anything you could dream up on your own. Just surrender. Surrender completely! Stop resisting and let Him take control.

God, what do You want us to know?

Let's embrace this adventure together!

For More Information

Visit

TellThemAnyway.com

www.ingramcontent.com/pod-product-compliance
Lightning Source LLC
Chambersburg PA
CBHW061706120626
46550CB00003B/1116